BIS Publishers
Het Sieraad
Postjesweg 1
1057 DT Amsterdam
The Netherlands
T (+) 31 (0)20-515 02 30
F (+) 31 (0)20-515 02 39
info@bispublishers.nl
www.bispublishers.nl

ISBN 978-90-6369-340-4
Second printing 2013
Third printing 2014

Written by: Susie Breuer
www.co-lab54.com
Designed by: Lilian van Dongen Torman
www.lilianvandongentorman.nl

Susie Breuer

.blue is the new black

The 10 Step Guide to Developing and Producing a Fashion Collection

BIS Publishers

FOREWORD
by Mariëtte Hoitink

"This book is an absolute must-read for everyone working in fashion or with ambitions to do so."

This book is an absolute must-read for everyone working in fashion or with ambitions to do so. In my daily work as the managing director of HTNK – the Amsterdam based premier fashion recruitment & consultancy agency – I get applications from people all over the world who want to make it big in fashion. Ever since the start of the 'Next Designer' or 'Models' television shows, a lot of people discovered their own inner designer star within themselves. In the eyes of the general public, fashion appears to be equivalent to glamour, but what a lot of people don't know is that this may well be the most intensive, life-consuming, demanding business there is. As a result, the fashion business is filled with people with extreme persistence, vision and talent, and therefore, it is indeed a lot of fun to work in, but definitely not for the reasons most people may think.

This book presents a practical overview, basic but detailed, of the heart of every fashion company: development and production. These are in most cases the teams that work together most intensively with all other departments – from design to legal, sales and marketing. This obviously makes this book a Bible for everyone with ambitions for careers in the buying, product development, and of course, production area. But they are not the only ones for whom this is relevant; for all those fashion professionals who work in design, marketing, sales, CSR, legal and financial departments, this book will provide some insight into why they occasionally find their production colleagues reaching their boiling points, running through corridors screaming and banging their heads against walls. Now they will know that the moment has come to hand

Mariëtte Hoitink

over that chocolate bar, bring some good coffee and take that head massage thingy out of its drawer. Your colleagues need you now.

Considering all the 'Green is the new black' slogans people keep throwing around nowadays, this book can create an understanding, a deeper awareness of where clothing comes from. I would like to believe that if people knew more about where exactly garments come from and how much effort and work has been put into their creation, they will treat them differently. From that perspective, I would highly recommend the general reader curious about clothes to give this book a go as well.

So, why is this book this relevant for such a large group of people? Because it hasn't existed before. Fashion is an industry that really lacks the documented methodology found in many other industries. This is so in spite of the fact that clothing is a basic

need; people all over the world deal with clothing every day and the industry has a significant influence on several countries' economies, environments and everyday life. I think, therefore, it is our job to invest in this industry's innovations that will turn the negative aspects of this business into positive ones. Innovation can only exist when information and methods are shared and discussed. Therefore, I'm very honoured to have met this most dedicated and talented fashion professional, Susie Breuer, who found the courage and extreme persistence to document this whole process, the core of every fashion company, whilst continuing to carry on her demanding job as a consultant for one of the most high end – and demanding – designer labels in the world. Huge respect.

Congrats,

Mariëtte Hoitink,
HTNK Fashion recruitment & consultancy
www.htnk.nl

PREFACE

Like most girls, I became interested in fashion at a fairly early age, tearing pages out of glossy magazines and learning how to use a sewing machine, but unlike most girls who are content to remain on the outside of the industry as a consumer, I decided to venture inside to become part of the global business of bringing fashion to the people.

Starting in the business at the humblest level, I have, over the years, worked in various roles in a wide range of companies, always learning on the job, often making mistakes, though seldom the same one twice, whilst experiencing the highs and the lows involved in the process of turning a designer's ideas into reality.

On countless occasions I wished that there was a book where I could look to find out what to do next, and how to do it, but there never was. As my experience grew and I became more and more senior in the business, watching assistants struggle with the same difficulties I had years ago, I realised that such a book was needed and that, perhaps, I had the breadth of experience to take on the task. Before doing so, I looked to see what was already in print, and found that whilst there

are many books about fashion, there still isn't a book available that gives the full, detailed picture of the whole process, that sets out in detail who does what, and in what order these have to be done for the process to work. I recognised the gap in the market and set about trying to fill it.

This book is written from my own personal experience of developing and producing fashion collections from high street brands to a catwalk line, and includes all the steps that are needed to turn the designer's sketch into a garment. It sets out the roles of all the people involved, the terms people use and the different responsibilities that rest with the people in various positions; in short, it is a step by step guide to developing a collection. In writing the book I considered it awkward to use 'they' when talking about a single

Susie Breuer

individual, so I have allocated male or female personal pronouns randomly to people performing various roles/functions, but I want to make it clear that any role/function can be performed by persons of either sex.

With every brand having its own method of working depending on its location in the world and their resources, it is hard to anticipate every different scenario that a developer or production coordinator may be faced with; however, what you will find in this book are the basic ideas that can help you understand the bigger picture of how a collection is made, and to help you find your way through the job and the industry as a whole. Development or production is not especially glamorous, but they are absolutely essential to the success of the process. It is no exaggeration to say that these departments are the linchpin of the creation of a fashion collection; without the tireless efforts of these people, invisible from outside the organisation, the collection simply would not be made.

The book has been written both as a guide to be read from cover to cover and as a reference book to be kept close to hand to be consulted as and when necessary. It might not tell the reader exactly how company x manages a certain procedure, but it provides the basic framework that makes the procedure at company x understandable. Although there is considerable variation between companies in job titles, management structures and chains of responsibility, what needs to be done to turn a design on paper into a garment on somebody's back, is pretty much the same everywhere.

Developing and producing a collection is extremely hard. It takes patience, determination and flexibility, but it is also one of the most rewarding aspects of the industry with the mix of creativity and problem solving. I hope this book helps to demystify the procedures and terminology and encourages more people to take this route into the industry.

ABOUT
this book

Fashion is a multi billion-dollar industry. It is not just about sketching an outfit, it is about selecting fabric, developing buttons, sourcing a factory, negotiating prices, making patterns, seeing to the final launch, and selling garments. It is a multi-faceted industry that is exciting, enigmatic and endless.

With many fashion schools now recognising the importance of including technical modules to their degrees, this guide is the perfect accompaniment to the relevant modules with its vocational A to z approach of what happens in the workplace, including how to build and maintain key business relationships.

People who buy *Blue is the New Black* want to know how to create a collection. They want to roll up their sleeves and do it, but they need practical instruction on the different stages. They don't want to read about data management systems or new thread developments; they want to understand what a range plan is and how to review a prototype with a factory.

Written for fashion graduates, fledgling entrepreneurs or those in entry level positions within the industry, this book demystifies the process of how to make a fashion collection, making it accessible for all levels. It is a reference guide, a buddy, and a Bible of who, what and where.

I

Chapter 1: **The Workings of the Fashion Industry**

This book is written specifically to deal with the functions and responsibilities of the developer and the production coordinator. It is aimed at anyone who wants to break in to the industry in these roles, but also for those currently working for a brand, whether alone or in a team. The roles of the developer and the production coordinator are fundamental to the creation of any collection as they work closely alongside every team in the brand, ensuring that the collection is created, priced, constructed and delivered at the right time and to the right place.

14

THE ROLE OF THE DEVELOPER/PRODUCTION COORDINATOR

If you are a developer or a production coordinator you usually need to anticipate problems and have the solutions ready before they arise, and to be that problem solver, you need you need to be analytical and organized.

You don't have to be a total number cruncher to succeed, but you do need to be comfortable with numbers, understand their relevance and how to use them. With so much information changing through every stage of the creation, you must have an organized mind to cope. Make plenty of lists, spreadsheets and tables with filters to keep on top of everything. Working with creative teams and factories can be exciting as well as infuriating. Learning how to negotiate with people as well as prices is an asset. Negotiating with a designer to keep the cost price of a style low whilst maintaining his vision is hard but rewarding. Colours, garments and fabrics change almost every day during development, so be flexible about change and open to new ideas and ways of working.

Last but not least, have an eye for detail. In both development and production, looking at every small detail of garments, prints and fabrics is key. It is your job to notice the flaw in the fabric, the shade difference in a colour, or the fact that on a sample one sleeve is longer than the other.

OTHER ROLES IN THE TEAM

Every fashion company is different when it comes to job titles, but there are certain key roles in every company that are needed to develop a fashion collection.

In general, a brand is made up of four areas of expertise:

> **design,**
> **development,**
> **production and**
> **merchandising.**

In short, the designer designs the collection, the developer is the link between the designer and the factory, the production coordinator makes sure the collection is made and delivered, and the merchandiser is in charge of the financial part of the business.

In order to understand in detail the parts played by all these in the creation of a collection and how their roles relate to each other, here is a short overview of their interrelationships.

DESIGN
The designer designs the garments, prints and embroideries for the collection. Together with the developer, he will also select the colours and fabrics for the garments and he is involved in the sample reviews. Once the collection has been made, the designer assists in creating the selling tools to help the sales team sell the clothes. The various job titles in different brands that deal with these tasks are: design director, design manager, junior designer, graphic designer, print designer and design assistant.

Some companies have dedicated concept designers whose job it is to define the design direction most suitable for the range, brand or company. Their specific job is to research the brand to form a new direction for the new season's collection. This means following trend forecasters, fabric mills, music trends, lifestyle trends, previous catwalk shows and current street fashion. If it isn't financially viable to have a specific concept designer, the designer can define the concept.

DEVELOPMENT
The developer in a fashion company is the link between the designer and the factories that will mass-produce the garments. From the start of the season he helps the designer in selecting fabrics and colours, while also keeping an eye on the financial side of things with the merchandiser. When the designs are ready, the developer conveys the designer's wishes to the factory so they can make a sample. The developer and the others in the brand review this sample and give their feedback. The factory can now adjust and improve the sample until the developer and designer are happy with the end result. When all samples for the collection are finalized, the developer's job ends with helping to organise a launch, where the samples are presented to sales teams.

Within the area of development functions the various job titles in different brands can be: development director, product development manager, product developers, development assistant, fabric manager, senior product manager, product manager and category manager.

PRODUCTION
The production coordinator works closely with the developer to take the collection from launch through production

to when the garments leave the factory. She arranges production fittings and production planning and manages the final pricing, order quantities and bulk lead times with the factory. During production she will travel to the factory to check the quality of the garments and packaging. Functions that deal with the production of a fashion collection are production director, production / sourcing manager, production coordinator and quality control assistant.

MERCHANDISING

The merchandiser is in charge of the financial part of the business and works together with both the developer and the production coordinator. He sets the pricing structure for the collection, makes sure the brand makes a profit, and makes adjustments to the collection according to feedback from the sales teams. When the samples are approved, he works with the production coordinator and the factories to finalise the prices and delivery dates of the garments and then issues the purchase order. The various job titles with this responsibility are: merchandise director, merchandise manager, merchandise and buy manager, merchandise and buy planner, merchandise assistant.

Three other roles you might encounter in the industry are the pattern maker, the members of the sales team and the branding manager.

PATTERN MAKER

Pattern makers are technically trained designers who create paper patterns from sketches. Their job is to translate the sketch of the designer into an actual garment by applying the base measurements and calculations. Throughout the stages of development and production they also

work alongside the factory, development and production team with the garment fittings. Pattern makers can also be called fit technicians.

SALES TEAM

The members of the sales team sell the finished collection to their customers, who can be international buyers, large department stores or small boutiques. Since they are connected to the stores and the buying public, the sales teams can inform the merchandiser about seasonal shifts in local sales trends so they can action adjustments in production if necessary. People who are selling a range can be called a sales manager or sales agent.

BRANDING MANAGER

The branding manager works for a branding or trims company, and develops new labels, buttons and badges for the brand to use on their garments. When dealing with branding, you will most certainly work with account managers.

SEASONS AND BUSINESS MODELS

In the past fashion companies presented new collections twice a year, in Autumn/ Winter (Fall) and Spring/Summer. Nowadays new collections are launched every few months with Pre Fall, Holiday, Pre Spring and Summer, providing smaller collections to keep the customers shopping. All of these collections follow the same sequence of design, development, merchandising, sales and production, which means that all the teams are working every week, often juggling more than one 'season' at a time, to bring new fashion to the stores.

Season	Launched	In store
Fall Season	January	July/September
Winter / Pre-spring Season	May	November/January
Spring Season	June	January/February
Summer / Pre-fall Season	October	March/April

Season	Launched	In store
Fall Season	March	July/September
Winter Season	May	September/October
Pre-spring Season	June	November/January
Spring Season	August	January/February
Summer Season	November	March/April
Pre-fall Season	January	May/June

In some cases business models in the industry follow the same timelines on, structure and procedure, but in other cases they are vastly different. Let's have a look at the two main business models, wholesale lines and retail lines to see how they differ.

WHOLESALE LINES

A wholesale line is bought by department stores or small independent shops throughout the year who sell it to the general public. This line can have between two and six collections a year (Pre Fall, Fall, Holiday, Pre Spring, Spring and Summer). Generally, with wholesale, the brand will design and make the collection at scheduled times of the year and then they will sell it to a department store, who will stock it in their stores with other wholesale brands.

RETAIL LINES

A retail line is for retail outlets only. This could, for example, be a high street chain, or maybe a brand that has its own stores. A retail line also launches between two and six and collections a year, but the chain stores or brands add new styles and stock into the stores every month. With retail, the development process can be shorter and more reactive to the shop customer. If a style is selling well in stores, the retail brand can decide to expand the style with more colours and fabrics.

In this book I explain the stages from the start of development to the end of production of one season. All these stages are relevant to both the retail and wholesale business models mentioned above, but in the discussion of timings in the text it is closer to the wholesale model than to the retail, where the timing of the various stages can vary enormously.

At the back of the book you can find a key dates calendar that gives you a simplified overview of when things happen and who does them. You can use it as a reference when reading this book, but also in your job in fashion.

Let me first explain in detail what will be discussed in this book.

FROM CONCEPT TO PRODUCTION

The starting point for any fashion collection has to be the concept. It is the foundation upon which a collection is created and it is an important reference point for the stages of development and production. A design team or concept designer can spend anything from 2 to 6 weeks creating the concept, looking for fabrics, selecting colours, finding photographic images that reflect a mood, and collecting ideas for the shape of garments. Chapter 2 is about this stage of concept creation and looks at how it can be constructed and what way it develops into a fashion collection. I will also briefly discuss what happens with the concept during the subsequent design stage.

At the same time as the concept is created, the merchandiser and developer construct the range plan. The range plan is a document listing all garments the collection will need to include in order to make a profit for the brand. If the concept is the backbone to the design, then the range plan is the backbone to merchandising and, like the concept, it is referred to regularly throughout the season. Chapter 3 describes the creation of a range plan and how it can be adjusted when changes to the collection occur during the development stage.

Once the range plan has been created, the designers, armed with their concept and range plan, start to design the collection, making sketches available for the developer. Working closely together now, the designer and developer also begin selecting fabrics and colours that work commercially for the garments. Chapter 4 deals both with fabric and colour selections and discusses how developers and designers at this stage often have to compromise to meet each other's goals. Fabrics and their characteristics are discussed in detail.

The information flow from the start of the development process to the end of production is a crucial element for the successful internal workings of the brand, and this is the subject of chapter 5. At the start of the design process the developer starts making the development matrix. This is the working document that is used to manage the development process from start to finish. It catalogues all the information relevant to the garments, such as the unique reference code, colour, fabric and style name. It is created and managed by one person and is updated daily, sometimes more often, to ensure that the development information is as complete and current as possible. Around 10 weeks into the process, the developer can start putting technical packs together. The technical packs are detailed documents that tell the factory exactly what the garments should look like. They contain a sketch, info about fabric and colour, a measurement chart, and details of the buttons, labels and threads for each of the garments designed.

The technical packs are handed over to the factories so they can make prototypes of the garments. The chapter on development and production information flow will discuss both information tools, but also production planning, and will explain when and how the development matrix eventually turns into the line list.

When the creation of the garments is in progress, the designer and the developer can start to have a look at the branding of the collection. Branding is a collective term for buttons, labels, hangtags, print artworks and embroidery designs, in fact anything that will carry the name of the brand inside or outside the garment. As with a garment, these take time to develop, so it is important to add them into the development process early. In chapter 6 I will discuss what constitutes branding, and how it is developed alongside (or just after) the garments.

When making a collection it is essential to have a reputable group of factories to make the garments. Some factories specialize in one or two types of products, while others can manage all types. In chapter 7 we will look at factories in all their forms. What factory types should you use? What relationships are there? How should you select the factories you want to work with? And most important of all, how do you get them to make the garment you want?

Based on their initial interpretation of the technical packs, the factories will supply you with prototypes of the garments. It is the developer's job to have the whole team review these prototypes and give feedback to the factories. According to the outcome of the review, the factory can either make a second prototype or go on to develop more detailed 'salesman' or production samples. These samples also need reviewing and the developer will once more pass on the result to the factory. The ins and outs of the reviewing stages are the subject of chapter 8. I will not only look at the implications of the different reviews, but will also offer advice on how to review effectively.

From the development, design and merchandising side, the launch of the collection is the goal towards which they have all been working. From this point on the sales teams of the brand start selling the range to different outlets and the success of the collection will become clear. The launch and the subsequent selling period are the subject of chapter 9. I will explain selling tools, like the line book and look book, and will also look at what happens with the feedback the sales teams get from their customers.

Finally, in chapter 10, I will take a brief look at themes you come across more and more: corporate social responsibility and sustainability.

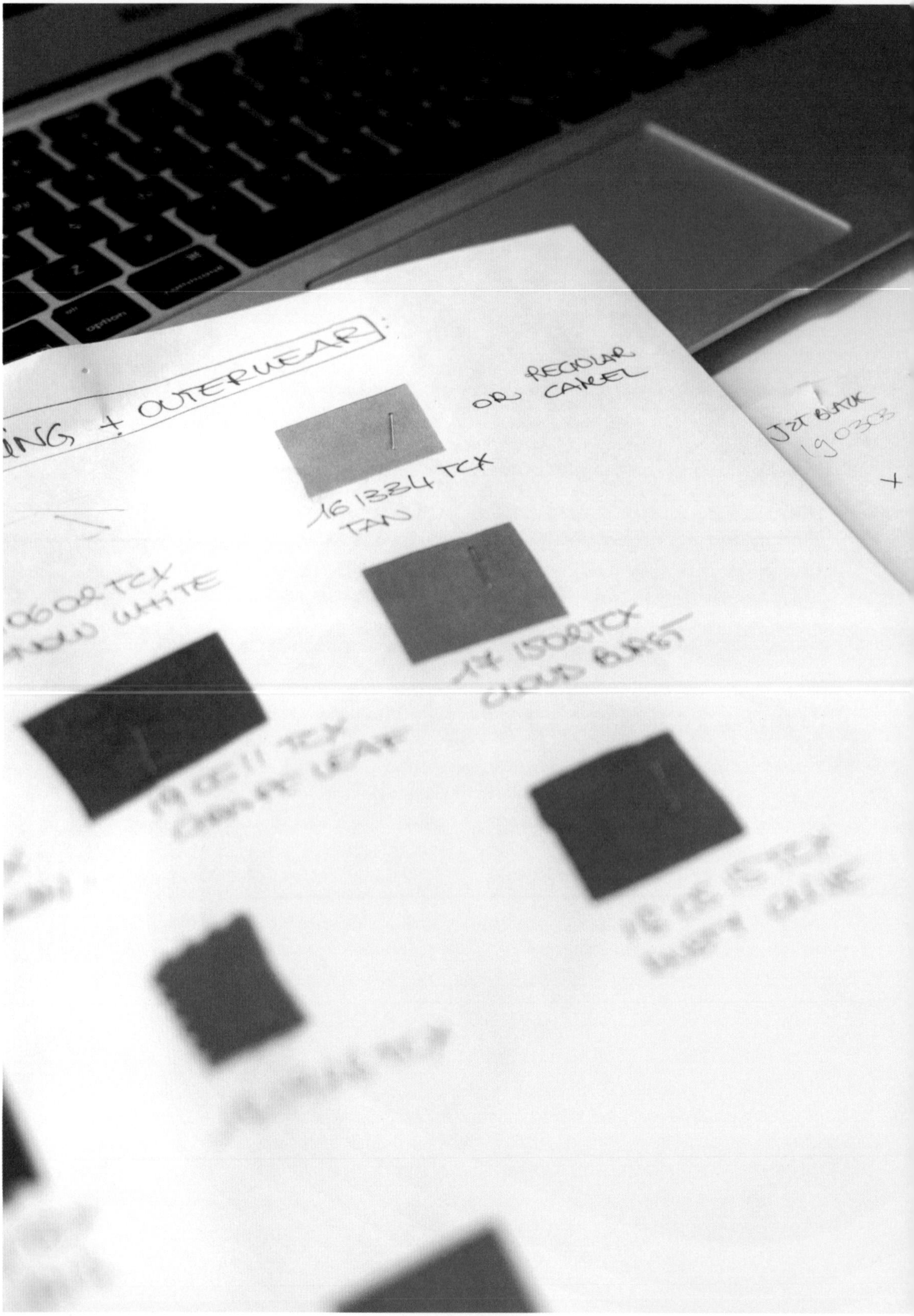

ING + OUTERWEAR

OR REGULAR OR CANCEL

JET BLACK
19 0303

X

16 1334 TCX
TAN

060R TCX
SNOW WHITE

17 1500 TCX
CLOUD BURST

19 0511 TCX
LEAF

16 0E 15 TCX

II

Chapter 2: **The Concept**

A brand stays in business by creating new collections every few months in the hope that customers will keep buying their clothes. In order to provide coherence to a collection, the brand needs a concept. It is the foundation upon which the collection is created and it is an important point of reference during the development, launch and production stages of the collection. Its generation can be the result of moments of inspiration or of careful analysis of market trends; in practice, both are important contributors to the formation of a successful concept.

WHAT IS A CONCEPT?

A concept is a design direction for the shape, colour, mood and fabric for any fashion collection, and is created at the beginning of the season. It creates the mood of the collection and is always open to different interpretations. The initial idea first needs to be analysed carefully and translated into something that people can actually look at, and that can set out the direction of the collection.

Several seasons ago the K Karl Lagerfeld launch concept was Rock and Roll Androgyny. The designer took images of androgynous models in skinny jeans and boyish clothes and built a men's and women's range around it. Black, white and grey were the colours, with an idea of using coated leather look fabrics, silver metallic prints and washed out, vintage look T-shirts. The starting point for the research was the love of denim and the colours, black and white, of Mr Lagerfeld himself. These three elements evolved into a concept that gave the feeling of rock and roll edgy clothes that could be worn by males and females.

A concept can come from fewer than three elements as well. A while ago, a spring collection for the Hilfiger Runway line had the theme: 'New York Country Club'. The concept began with the words Country Club, and from there, images of 60s and 70s women's sporting clothes, pleated tennis whites, halter neck tops and mini dresses were added to the visuals. Images of Katherine Hepburn in her signature high-waist wide leg pants matched with bra tops gave the movie star reference, and the fabrics for the mood were fine chiffons, and checked linens.

Mood images from magazines are pinned on a board to start the concept.

ELEMENTS OF A CONCEPT

The four parts of the concept are fabrics, colours, shapes and mood. We shall look at them in detail and explain what exactly they consist of and how they influence the process of development.

FABRIC
Fabrics (or yarns and textiles) are very important to the feeling of the concept. Most concepts are first presented in the form of a handful of fabric pieces. They provide a tangible expression of the feeling you want to convey. If you want to evoke a 1920s romantic, nostalgic feeling in a concept, chiffon would be perfect to conjure up an image. A men's military theme would have heavy weight cotton or boiled woolen fabric to illustrate the mood. Fabrics add an extra dimension to the concept, but they do not have to be the only ones used for the collection. It is, however, a signature element.

COLOUR
Sitting alongside the selection of fabrics is the composition of the colour palette. The palette is a collection of colours (or tones, tints, shades, hues, stain wash or dyes) that will be used throughout the range collection. Making a palette for a concept is not easy. The shades selected have to work not only in many of the types of garments but also in the colours of buttons, zips, prints and embroideries.

For instance, yellow is a bright and 'happy' colour – mostly used for spring and summer ranges. It is a good colour for a T-shirt or a pair of socks, but can you imagine it in a wool coat or a suit? It's a hard colour to have

© Amsterdam Fashion Institute, Individuals, Spring/Summer '08

24

it in a great mass, but in small portions or in a specific fabric it works. It is also great for small embroidery on the chest of a shirt, a print on a T-shirt, a raincoat, or even a chiffon dress, but it has to have its place. Navy, on the other hand, is a great suit or coat colour, as it is a classic shade that everyone can wear. It also works on trims (e.g. buttons and zips), but could be seen as boring or too 'classic' for a print or embroidery.

Experiment with fabrics to see what works together and what doesn't. Take one colour and two or more fabrics, decide which fabric has the stronger colour tone when compared to the others. Do they all work or is one a stronger element? It is a nice challenge to assemble the colour palette, making sure it ticks the above boxes, as well as being 'new' and interesting for another season.

SHAPE

Shapes within a concept refer to the sizing aspects of the garments in the collection, and every season the shape of garments changes for both men and women. In the early 70s the style for trousers was flared at the hem and tight at the waist and hip. In the late 70s there was the drainpipe jean that was super tight all over. In the 80s we had the power suit with the padded shoulder, and a decade later the shoulder lines got softer and less structured, giving a more relaxed look. These are just some important changes over decades, but even measurement variations of 5 cm can make a difference between seasons for a pair of high waist or waisted jeans. Being clear about the direction of the fit is vital for the concept.

LONG SLEEVE
SHIRT

5.

How to fit in, and you grow attached?

MOOD

The mood of the concept adds an emotional element to the concept that 'sets the scene' for the other elements. If we go back to the K Karl Lagerfeld concept, the mood would be signalled with images of rock and roll bands, confrontational shots of models with blunt cut hairstyles, dramatic make up and monochrome imagery. For the Hilfiger line there would be faded sunsets, sheer pastel-coloured fabrics, and nostalgic images of models, hair blowing in the breeze at a 50s American sporting Country Club.

WHO CREATES THE CONCEPT?

Some companies have concept designers whose job it is to define the design direction of the range, brand or company. Their specific job is to understand the brand's customer profile and heritage to form a new direction for the new season's collection. This means following trend forecasters, fabric mills, music trends, lifestyle trends, catwalk shows, graduate fashion shows and current street fashion to decide on a direction most suitable for their brand. If it isn't financially viable to have a specific concept creator, the designer can be entrusted to define the concept.

Details on a period dress can be used for inspiration.

IDEAS FOR THE CONCEPT

Ideas are everywhere. They can strike at any hour of the day or night, and any time of the year. This is why it is so important to be aware of all the possibilities that are around, that are heard, seen or read. Reading books, watching movies, people-watching, all raise questions about words, characters, clothes, colours and scenery, many of which can be a starting point for the development of a concept. Concepts are formed from the strangest, most random beginnings. Concept designers keep a notebook and camera with them at all times, taking notes and pictures of anything they see that might be of interest.

HISTORY

Historical references can play a huge role in fashion collections. Whether it is a fabric, a garment type or a whole silhouette, designers have been referencing history for years. John Galliano referenced Marie Antoinette in his 2010 collection, and Alexander McQueen alluded to his Scottish ancestry in his Highland Rape collection with tartan fabrics and heraldry. Military influences are always strong in menswear and even with denims; the history of work-wear has been researched and updated by many a denim company. There is such a phenomenal depth of information available for shapes, colours and fabrics that the options are endless, and what's more, it is free.

SHOPPING TRIPS

Every major shopping city in the world has interesting and innovative shops. Whether they are the international chains or small local independent stores, window-shopping in a new city can give inspiration on colours, shapes, fabrics and trim details. Shopping

28

at someone else's expense sounds like a pretty nice way to spend your time, and while I'm not going to try to pass it off as 'a hard business trip', it is a good way for the designer to increase the chances of picking up ideas. Staying in an office and trying to invent a new season is almost impossible, because of the day-to-day distractions, phone calls and meetings, but at the same time the reality of walking for eight hours in and out of stores whilst suffering from jet-lag, trying to make notes on styling details without being removed by in-store security is a tough challenge. The result is that whilst the shopping trips are nice, they are hard work, tiring and frustrating, but nevertheless essential. Don't forget the vintage shops for research. Charity shops and second hand stores are great for the small details on coats, bags and scarves. Many of the luxury labels shop at vintage stores for their inspiration.

STREET STYLE

People-watching and photographing what they are wearing is a great way of spotting new trends and styles. Spending time in a new city will open up a new world of local designers, local clubs, bars and cafes, all with creative people expressing themselves in what they are wearing and how they are wearing it. Small details, like a turn up on a pair of jeans, the neckline of a T-shirt or the length of a jacket can have an immediate impact on the newness of a garment. By using the internet to research the 'cool' areas of a city, and sitting in a cafe or bar, the designer obtains a huge amount of information, which can add excitement to the shapes, mood or colours of a concept.

Designers do as the forecasting companies do: they window-shop and people-watch. If they're working on a limited budget and

Street style: hanging out at a trade fair.

are unable to hit style hubs such as NYC, Tokyo, LA, Paris, London, Antwerp or Milan, they try something closer to home. Cities, such as those above, are hotbeds for new trends and styling. Getting away from your usual location will help you find different styles, shops and images.

TREND ANALYSIS

Trend forecasting these days is big business, with established companies all over the world working several years ahead on customer profiling, shopping habits, colour analysis and silhouette cycles, formulating analyses targeted for focused demographics, and presenting their results in websites, books, seminars and trade shows.

There isn't a designer or brand that doesn't use some kind of trend service. They put in the hours of research for you, giving brands the edited highlights in a purely visual display. They work to an international market with editors all over the world who visit shops and exhibitions, follow street trends, look at graduate shows and fabric fairs. There is no possible way that one person could have this much information at their fingertips at any one time. The yearly subscription to the services is expensive, but for any brand it should be a necessary cost.

WORKSHOPS
If money is no object, customised reporting can be commissioned by individual brands, but at the same time many trend companies are represented at the fabric and industry trade fairs with presentations and workshops offered to all participants.

Workshops at the industry trade fairs are free introductions to the trend company's services. They give examples of how they approach their research, and how it leads to useful and relevant information that can be bought. The workshops are usually split by market, so there are presentations on street fashion, and children's, men's and women's wear.

WEBSITES

Some websites that are highly used in the fashion industry are *www.mudpie.co.uk*, *www.wgsn.com* and *www.stylesight.com.* These have developed in order to cover every element of trend analysis from fabrics to colours, interiors, denim, junior, shoes, hats and garments. For a substantial fee,

shop reports can be obtained from major fashion hubs around the globe, giving colour indications for every denomination and age group, and shape analysis for every known product group.

A mid point between the above trend websites and doing the whole thing yourself are companies, such as Mode Information (*www.modeinfo.com*). Working across all markets and demographics, Mode Information produces trend books and reports each season, which can be used to guide a designer or buyer on colours, fabrics, yarns and also shapes.

Just one of the halls at the
Bread&Butter trade fair in Berlin.

DURING REVIEWS

The concept is the creative backbone of
the collection, and as a result it is used as
a reference at the key review stages. At
the proto review, launch and production
review stages it is essential to refer back to
the concept to ensure that the vision of the
designer remains evident. With changes
happening all the time on colour, fabric
and fit, the developer and the designer will
always need to be aware of the concept, and
will question the link of the product of the
moment to the concept before proceeding.

For instance, if one of the fabrics in the
concept was a silver leather, it would be
important to have that leather in at least

three of the garments in the collection, as
well as being used as a colour on a printed
T-shirt and, perhaps, an embroidery on a
shirt. This way the silver aspect is carried
through the range. If in the proto review the
silver print is cancelled and the embroidery
changed to a purple colour, then we
immediately have a problem, as we have
lost some links to the concept. If, when we
get to the production stage, we find that
the orders for the silver fabric are not high
enough and the leather is cancelled, we
have lost every aspect of the key colour that
was in the concept. By referring back to the
concept at each key stage we can question the
changes, so ensuring the concept stays intact
throughout development and production.

llectieShoot

Styling

- -

Understanding how elements of a concept influence
a range is very important for the developer. Watch how
the designer works and ask questions to get a clear
understanding.

Not every colour in the colourcard is used for a fabric,
some are just used for trims, but they are still important
to the range.

Having a personal interest in fashion and trends will
help you with design and style references, which will
be used throughout the creative process.

Don't be afraid to offer up ideas for colour and fabric
sourcing. Developing a range is a collaborative process.

Try to keep a copy of the concept with you throughout
the development process so that you have a constant
reference point and reminder.

- -

III

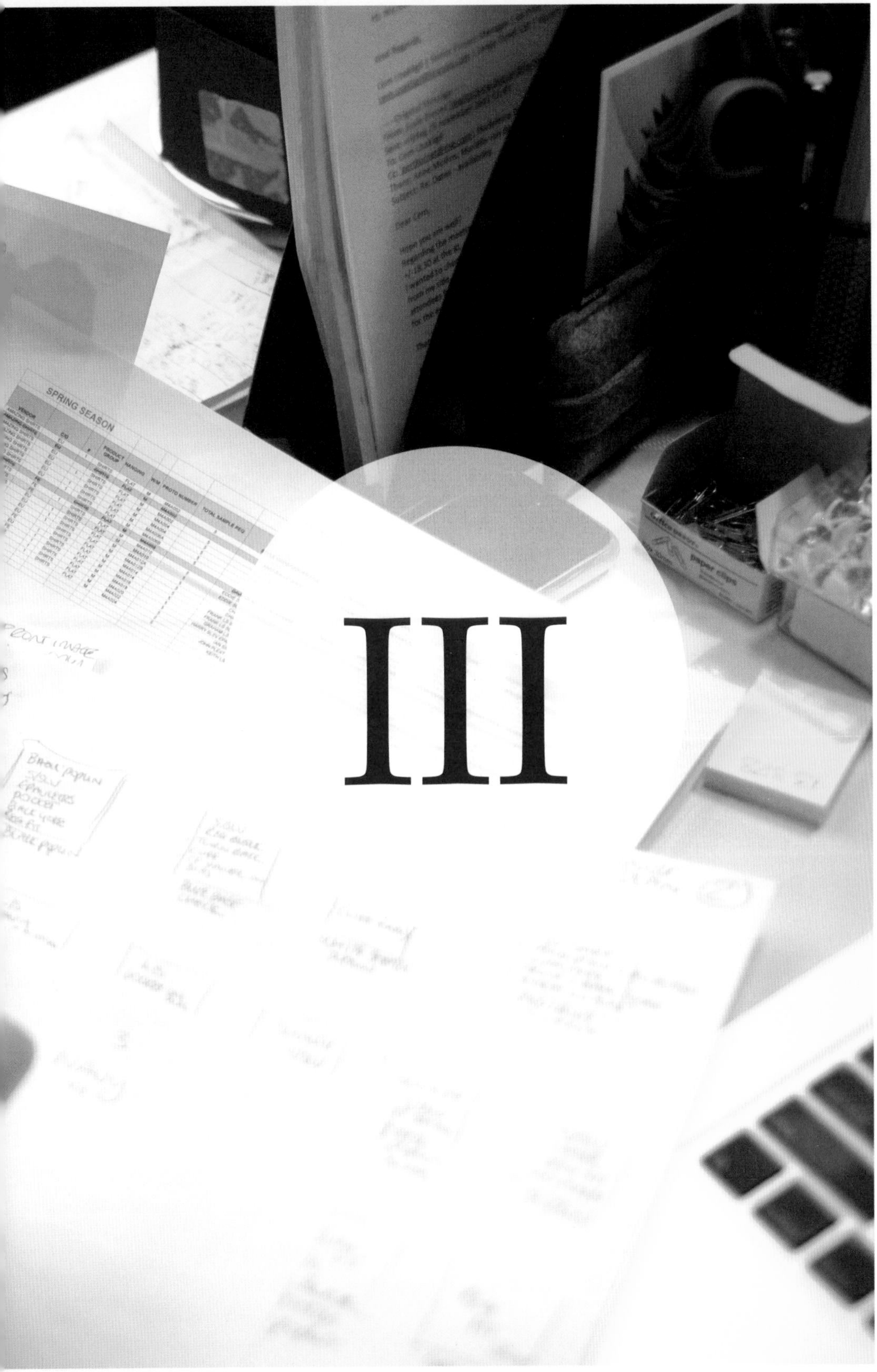

Chapter 3: **Range Planning**

From a developer's perspective, the basis for any fashion collection is the range plan. It is a table of information listing the quantity and type of garment styles to be planned and designed for the collection of a specific season. The merchandise team and development team create it jointly, and its construction is guided by the previous season's sales.

In smaller companies there may be only a single person making the range plan, but in larger companies the designer, the fashion buyer or financial people can have input too. Each person contributing to the range plan approaches it with a different objective. The merchandise team looks to the financial side, the developer to the technical aspects of the garments, and if there is a separate designer involved, he will look at the conceptual side of the plan.

WHAT DOES A RANGE PLAN LOOK LIKE?

In most companies, a range plan is a chart laid out in a grid with columns and rows. Often the range plan is created in MS Excel, but there is plenty of software designed especially for range planning. Pen and paper can be used as well, but you should be able to keep updating the document, so it is better to use an electronic format. There is a list of tips for relevant software in the back of this book. In some companies the range plan is also displayed on the wall of an office making it easier to physically move the sketches around the board as the fabric is selected for them until the final decisions have been made. Providing you have the physical space, this is a great way to visualize the range as it evolves and bring the Excel range plan to life. If you don't have the space for a wall plan, a miniature version can be created in MS Excel, which is called a merchandise plan. This holds the same information as the range plan, but has small sketches instead of X-s to illustrate the styles.

Denim

	99	129	149	200	
Pants					
Mid: Skinny	x				
Mid: Straight		x			
Mid: Wide leg		x			
Top: Fashion piece			x		
Skirt					
Basic	x				
Top: Fashion piece		xx			
Dress					
Basic			x		
Top: Fashion piece				xx	

Leathers

	299	349/399	449	599	699
Basic: Biker jacket		/x	x		
Mid: Field jacket			x		
Top: Fashion piece	x			x	x
Vest		x/			

Light Weight Jersey

	49	59	79	99	129/149
Tops					
Basic: Long sleeve	x	x	x		
Basic: Tank	x				
Top: Fashion piece			x	x	x/x
Dresses					
Basic			x	x	
Top: Fashion piece			x	x	/x

Sweater Knits

	79	99	129	189/199	229
Basic	xx	x			
Mid: Fine gauge	x	x	x	x	
Top: Fashion piece			xx	x/x	x

COMPONENTS

Below I will list the components in order of importance.

PRODUCT GROUPS

In the image on the left page you see the product groups listed from top to bottom: denim, leathers, light weight jersey and sweater knits. These product groups can be either groups of garments that have the same features and fulfill the same clothing need of the customer (outerwear; pants), or they can be groups of items made of the same material (leather; denim). If the product group is a material type (like denim or leather), it should be subdivided further into garment types.

> **Outerwear**
  (jackets, coats, blazers.)
> **Suits**
  (matching jacket, pants, skirts – can be soft, like floaty light fabric or structured formal suit.)
> **Dresses**
  (day dress or ball gown.)
> **Woven bottoms**
  (trousers, shorts, denim, non-denim, skirts.)
> **Woven tops**
  (blouses, shirts, fashion tops.)
> **Sweater knits**
  (sweaters made from wool, cashmere or cotton, but generally, knitted either by hand or by machine.)
> **Sweats**
  (sweatshirts)
> **Jersey**
  (T-shirts, draped jersey tops, rib vests.)
> **Accessories**
  (hats, scarves, gloves, bags, ties, shoes, belts.)

GARMENT TYPES

The garment types making up the product groups are listed in the left hand column shown in bold type. For example, the product group denim consists of pants, skirts and dresses. Some product groups are self-explanatory and do not need to be divided further (i.e. sweater knits).

STYLES

Below the garment types in the left column, each type is divided further into individual pieces of clothing, called styles. These styles sometimes convey information about material (short wool coat) or sometimes they indicate a certain fit (skinny denim, wide leg denim).

SELLING PRICES

Moving on to the second to the sixth column, you will see the selling prices of the product groups. I will explain later on how these prices come into existence, but for now, note that prices within a range are determined right from the start of the development process. Usually, the designs are made accordingly. The crosses in the cells defined by the garment styles (rows) and the prices (columns) show exactly how many different styles in each garment will be for sale at what price.

WHEN IS THE RANGE PLAN CREATED?

The key dates calendar shows that the range plan is created right after the concept for the collection has been established, very much at beginning of the process. It is important to remember that the development of a collection is a continuing process and that the range planning for one season overlaps with the later stages of the production process of the previous season's collection. So, the feedback the sales teams give from the

Creating a range plan on the wall.

previous seasons influences the development of the new range plan. From here on, the range plan dictates what the new range is going to look like.

BASIC, MID AND TOP STYLES

Within the list of styles on the left you will also see the words basic, mid and top mentioned. Within their product group, garments are either a basic, mid or top style. The styles of a garment reflect directly their cost price, selling price and use of material.

In this instance let's look at a range of socks from basic to top layer. Think of a product group as a pyramid with three layers. The lowest layer is the base of the collection. This has all the safe styles that are sold month on month, year on year. They provide the regular income for the company and could be, in this case, the plain black sock or the plain white sport sock. Nothing fancy about it, but always reliable and needed all year round.

The next layer is something a little more expensive, and would be styles that are more colourful, maybe with stripes or a fancy pattern. Thinking about the customer, maybe the same guy who buys the sport socks every few months would buy something striped or spotty for a weekend. This second layer adds interest to the range without being too crazy in design or too expensive. This layer can be updated regularly to keep the range in the shops interesting.

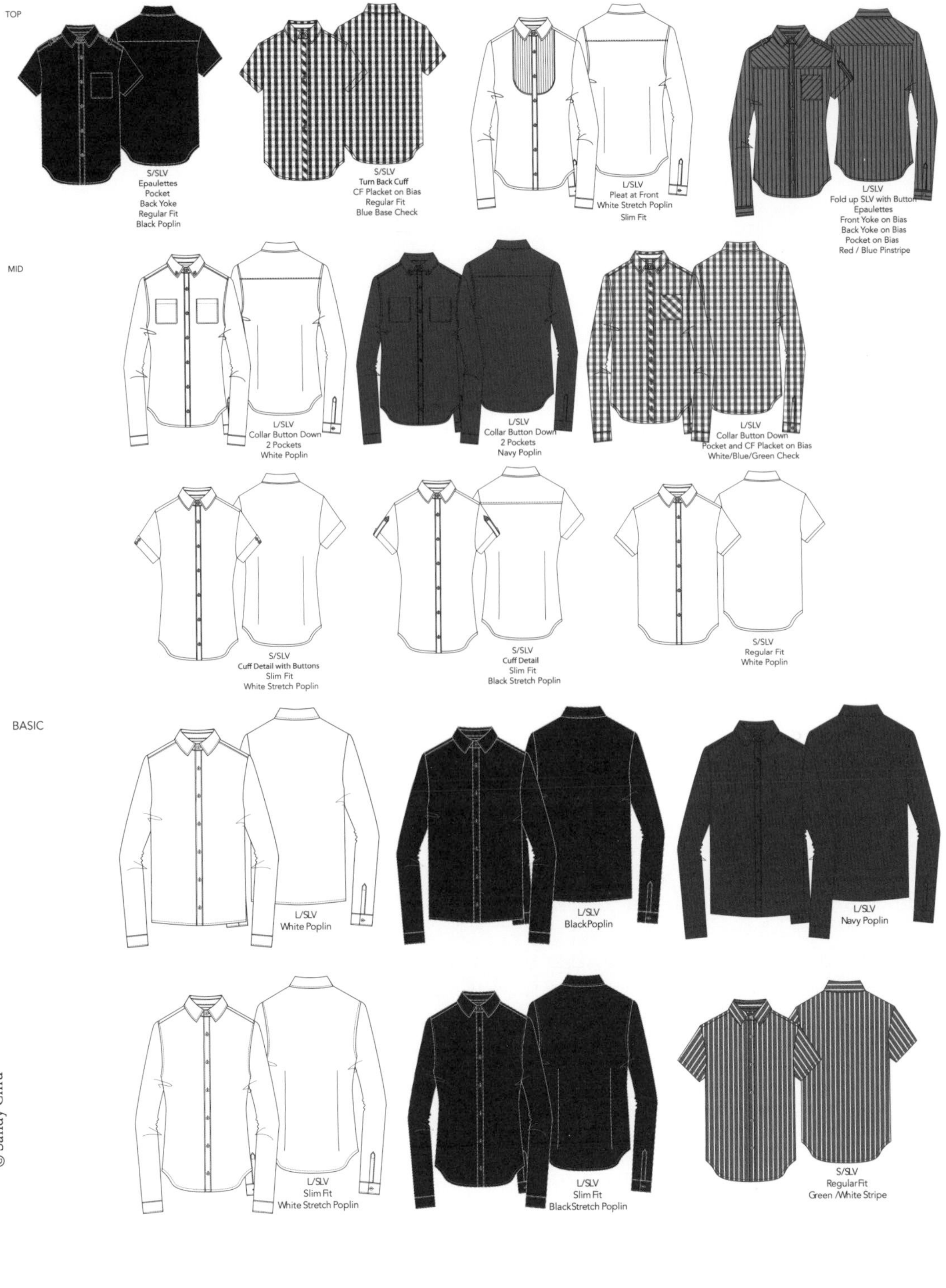

S/SLV
Epaulettes
Pocket
Back Yoke
Regular Fit
Black Poplin

S/SLV
Turn Back Cuff
CF Placket on Bias
Regular Fit
Blue Base Check

L/SLV
Pleat at Front
White Stretch Poplin
Slim Fit

L/SLV
Fold up SLV with Button
Epaulettes
Front Yoke on Bias
Back Yoke on Bias
Pocket on Bias
Red / Blue Pinstripe

MID

L/SLV
Collar Button Down
2 Pockets
White Poplin

L/SLV
Collar Button Down
2 Pockets
Navy Poplin

L/SLV
Collar Button Down
Pocket and CF Placket on Bias
White/Blue/Green Check

S/SLV
Cuff Detail with Buttons
Slim Fit
White Stretch Poplin

S/SLV
Cuff Detail
Slim Fit
Black Stretch Poplin

S/SLV
Regular Fit
White Poplin

BASIC

L/SLV
White Poplin

L/SLV
Black Poplin

L/SLV
Navy Poplin

L/SLV
Slim Fit
White Stretch Poplin

L/SLV
Slim Fit
Black Stretch Poplin

S/SLV
Regular Fit
Green /White Stripe

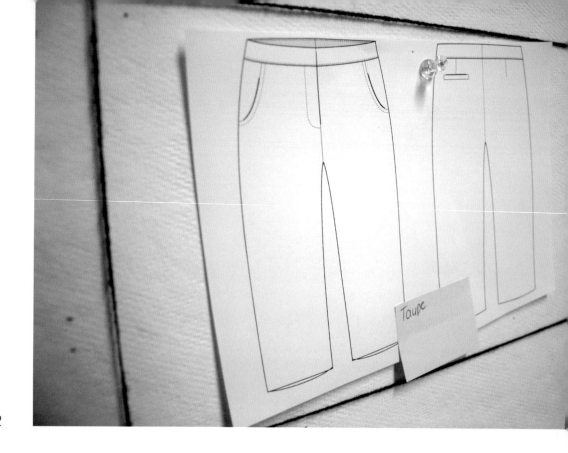

The top layer is really the aspirational style in the range. It is the sock that is made from cashmere or silk, has a crazy colour or pattern, and is understandably, more expensive. We call this aspirational because the customer who buys the regular black sock 'aspires' to the concept of wearing the cashmere sock all the time, but in reality his budget and lifestyle may not allow it. It is crucial for the range to have this top layer, as season on season this top layer will slowly move down the pyramid to the middle layer and will be replaced with a new aspirational design.

The style of the garment dictates the cost price, selling price and materials used. Since there are three levels of quality of the socks, there should also be a clear price difference between them. The basic sport sock is the lowest price point, followed by the striped sock and ending in the cashmere sock. The quantities produced would follow this pyramid model: more at the basic level or entry point and fewer at the top.

FACTORS

Most small companies will determine the quantity, colour, fit and price of the range without looking at a more detailed analysis, while large brands look at trend forecasting, financial history, local market feedback, target revenue requirements and brand heritage. As a company grows in size, the variety of input into the range plan will grow too. Here's a more detailed look at the factors that determine the content of the range plan.

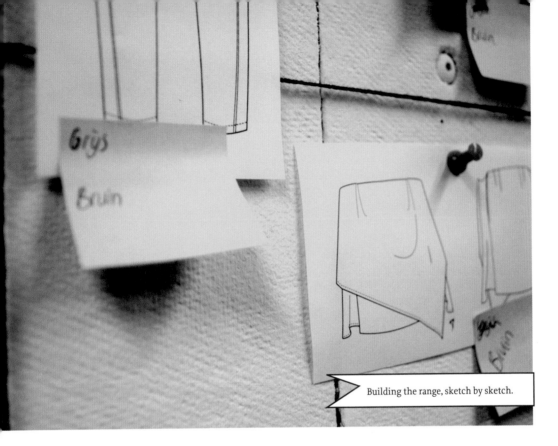

Building the range, sketch by sketch.

SALES HISTORY

The history of sales relates to the previous season's best and worst sellers. Most ranges have best sellers every season, and at the start of planning, the merchandise team refers back to the previous season's sales figures. In order to capitalise on sales, the best sellers are recoloured or refabricated to make them look newer. These are added to the range plan by the merchandise team, and are placed as a 'basic' or 'mid style' in each of the product groups. These are usually at the lowest or the middle price for the brand, and are a platform to which the more fashionable and higher priced styles are added. To the customer it looks like a new style, as it is in a different colour or fabric, but to the brand it is an easy sale and one upon which a range can be built.

Some brands are well known for their classic heritage styles that recur in their collection year on year. During the range planning, the merchandiser would look at the brand history to plan in a quantity of these classic heritage styles. Have you ever seen a Burberry collection without trench coats? Probably not, and it is because the merchandiser made sure to include them.

PRICE

By looking into the sales history of the previous season you can also get an understanding of the effective and less effective price points. If you have a selection of T-shirts that are for sale, and the prices are at 49€, 59€, 69€ and 129€, you have three price points close to each other in value and then a gap before the next one. If you

© Amsterdam Fashion Institute, Individuals, Autumn/Winter '10

Illustrations and technical sketches reviewed against the range plan.

compare this to our pyramid structure, it would be hard to make three tiers out of these prices, as three are too close to each other and the last one is too high in comparison. When analyzing the sales, the merchandise team may see that price points 49€, 69€ and 129€ are effective for the consumer, but at 59€ nothing sells. In this case they would, for the next season, keep the 49€ for the basic style, change the 69€ to 79€ for the mid price style and keep the 129€ as the top price, so that there was a more logically spaced set of prices. The merchandiser would reanalyse the prices the following season to see the effect of the change, and this in turn would affect the next season's prices.

SHAPE

The analysis of garment shapes from previous seasons should affect the key shapes that the designer uses. For instance, the merchandiser has seen that in the spring collection there was a women's short trench coat that had a great sales order, and they think that it is also a style that can be carried over to the winter season just by changing the fabric to a heavier weight. The merchandiser adds this into the range plan as a 'carry over' style, and the designer researches fabrics for this updated style. By recognizing the strength of a shape, the brand can capitalize on previous seasons styles and the customer who loved the coat in the spring, can also buy a version for the winter as the fabric is warmer.

COLOUR

Colour analysis is vital each season and helps the designers determine its use in the collection. The merchandiser and designer work closely to determine the end use of all the colours in the concept. The colours the designer adds to his concept need to work not only for the fabrics, but also for the prints, embroideries and trims of the collection. Fluorescent pink maybe a 'hot' colour for the season, as predicted by the trend forecasters, but sales analysis by the merchandiser has shown that for a men's range the pink doesn't work in a fabric, but only in a print or embroidery.

FINANCIAL TARGETS

The merchandise team is in charge of the prices and the financial side of the range plan, so at the start of the season they have a total figure of what the brand needs to make in profit for the season. By looking at the previous season's sales they know that in order to make this profit they need to have ten coat styles selling at 200€ and seven jacket styles at 150€, etc. With this information the merchandise and development teams break down the range plan by product group and selling price, so that the designer knows precisely what needs to be designed. The developer works closely with the designer at this stage to calculate target cost prices for the factory and to align the sketches to the range plan, making sure that it is technically possible to make the coat for the required selling price.

LOCAL MARKET FEEDBACK

Merchandisers would look to their sales agents to obtain locally based feedback on their best and worst sellers, as well as relevant local trends. Think of local trends, the climate, cultural influences and styling, and you can understand the need for market relevance.

Be aware that there is a fine line between taking on board local market feedback and being true to your brand's identity. Ignoring a market request can kill sales and collaboration, but being a slave to the market dilutes the brand identity and causes confusion for the customer. A possible solution for this is to create market-specific packages of styles that sit alongside the regular collection; this way sales are maximised, the brand has a clear message and it stays focused and relevant while serving local customers.

If you are building a brand identity, stay true to what the identity is. Take into consideration what the market is asking, and if you can make the request without straying from your identity do it, but don't sell out and try to be all things to all people.

TRUE STORY

- -

I once worked for a brand that had a black and white colour palette. At the launch of the first collection (which was a very small range), one of our sales team, who was based in a warm sunny country, requested one of the T-shirts to be produced in pink, as this is what her customers would buy (based on the colours of other successful brands). She built a strong case for the added colour, but in the end we

said no, and the T-shirt remained in black and white. Why? Simple. We were building a brand identity, the colour scheme was monochrome, it was a small range and the addition of the pink T-shirt would a) look strange and b) confuse the customer. We were not in a position to add the colour just for this market, as we would have had production minimum issues.

- -

COMPILING A RANGE PLAN

Now that you know what a range plan generally looks like, let's see how you can compile one yourself for either your own company or collection or the brand you are working for. In this 'how-to' I will assume you are working with an Excel file, but if you rather work with pen and paper for now, that's also OK.

If I were to create a range plan I would start with a sheet of paper and would write across the top the type of garment, for instance, coats. You can use any product group you want.

Under that, write horizontally across the page the required/proposed selling prices. The merchandiser will give you these prices from the previous season's sales history. Let's fill in six selling prices for the coats: 159€ / 199€ / 249€ / 299€ / 349€ and 399€. Sometimes there are more selling prices and sometimes fewer, it is company and product group specific.

Once you have written out the type of garment (coats) and the prices, you need to decide how many styles are actually needed. The merchandiser can give you this number based on the financial targets of the company. They would calculate that, for instance, the company would need nine coat styles distributed between six different prices to make enough money for the season. Write down on the left hand side of the sheet, coat 1, coat 2, etc. until you have nine lines down the page.

Using sales analysis and local market feedback, the merchandiser can now tell you that out of the nine coat styles, there need to be four simple looking styles, three need to be a little more fancy and the rest should be super fashionable crazy designs that will get PR attention.

The merchandiser could also tell you that, since your top sales markets are Sweden and Spain, you need to make sure some of the coats have a hood for Sweden, as it gets cold there, while some of the others should have ¾ sleeves, as this is a great feature in Spain. At least one of the styles could be the same as last season with a different fabric, but the rest of them should be new styles. Under no circumstances can the coat be in a velvet fabric, as this would never sell for the brand.

Now that all the blanks are filled in, you can go to the designer to tell him that he needs to design nine coats, four of which are more simple styles, three have more detail and two that are very detailed. They need to include a best seller from last season, and some of the styles must have a hood.

If the designer will 'reuse' or 'carry over' a trench coat from last season that sold for 199€; you can already add this style into the range plan by writing Coat 1 – Trench coat, and putting an X under the price point of 199€. One style is now taken.

Continue filling up the plan for coats until you have detailed coat descriptions and fit information down the left of the page from the designer with X-s under all the price points. Move onto the next type of garment until your plan is complete.

- -

As the developer, the range plan is your starting point of a new season. Watch and learn from the merchandiser.

At the early stages, the range plan will change a lot in respect of prices and number of styles. Be patient and flexible.

Some designers 'over sketch' by up to 50% on the number of styles compared to the requirements of the range plan. If you see this happening, raise a red flag and be sure to keep raising it at the proto review where the number can be reduced.

Make sure there is a clear price build up for each product group. If you see a gap of more than 3 price points between prices, this should prompt a question, as it means that the range plan isn't balanced. Don't be afraid to ask questions if something isn't clear or doesn't make sense.

Remember your end customer and pay attention to local market feedback; make sure it is covered in the range plan.

- -

PRICING INFORMATION
價格資料

MANDATORY

(est items)

ed
s to Laundering or Dry Cleaning
s to Crocking
s to Light
to Non-Chlorine Bleach
Non-exempt fabrics only. All colors)

Hong Kong

HKD 322

Test Method
AATCC 61
AATCC 8/ 116
AATCC 16 (20 Hours)
AATCC/ASTM TS-001
16 CFR 1610

(est items)

to Laundering or Dry Cleaning
s to Crocking
s to Light
to Non-Chlorine Bleach
ashed Garment, Washed De

Hong Kong

USD 52   HKD 40

Test Method
AATCC 61
AATCC 8/ 116
AATCC 16 (20 Hours)
AATCC/ASTM TS
AATCC 61

(est items)

Laundering or Dry Cleaning
ooking
ght
Non-Chlorine Bleach
nt Runs
empt Fabrics only, All colors)

Hong Kong

USD 51

Test Me

Chapter 4: **Fabrics**

Without fabric there would be no garment. You could have the best design in the world, but without fabric it can't be realized. Making a judgment call on which fabrics to use and for which garment is a skill, and it is one that can be learnt through experience in the workplace. For example, look at the clothes in your wardrobe. Take a cotton shirt and imagine what it would be like in a heavy wool fabric. Take a silk dress and imagine it in denim. Both the dress and shirt would still be wearable, but would probably be suitable for different occasions. Understanding which fabric is used for what style and why, is part of the skill of the developer.

FABRIC CHARACTERISTICS

There are thousands of different fabrics used, but for a starting point I will break them down into four categories: knitted fabrics, woven fabric, bonded/non-woven fabrics, and yarns.

COMPOSITION
The composition of the fabric is the mix of different yarns it is made from. It can be split into two sections, the first is natural fibres (cotton, linen, wool and silk), and the second is synthetic or artificial fibres (e.g. viscose, modal, polyester, nylon). Some fabrics are made of a single fibre, and some are blends of two or more fibres. The composition of the fabric affects the performance of the fabric in its end use. For instance, a shirt in 100% cotton will probably be creased when it is washed and will need to be ironed. The same shirt in 50% cotton 50% polyester probably

won't need to be ironed, as the long fibres of the polyester yarn help to keep the fabric flatter.

CONSTRUCTION
The construction of a fabric refers to how it is made. Some are woven, some are knitted and some are bonded. Under these headings the categories can be broken down into different weaves and knitting techniques. Here are some examples of the types of weaves and fabrics and their suitability for specific garments and product groups.

WOVEN
A woven fabric is constructed by weaving a warp and a weft thread together. The warp threads run along the length of the fabric and the weft from side to side. At the edge of the fabric on each side is the selvedge. Woven fabrics can made from both natural and

synthetic fibres and can be used for shirts, coats, jackets, dresses, pants and skirts. The three basic weave constructions are plain, twill and satin.

BONDED OR NON-WOVEN
Bonded fabrics are constructed by sealing together synthetic fibres by heat or adhesive. They are not as strong as woven fabrics, but can be used for interlinings for garments or in felted fabric, which can be used for hats or slippers.

JERSEY KNIT
Jersey knit is a knitted fabric, and is used for T-shirts or any lightweight knitted garments. Most jersey is made on a circular knitting machine, which means it is knitted in a seamless loop. Jersey knit doesn't have to

be in cotton; it can be in a variety of yarns. Common jersey qualities are: single jersey, double jersey or interlock.

SWEATER YARN
Sweater yarns are also knitted into garments, but here they describe sweaters rather than T-shirts. Sweater yarns can be of natural, synthetic or metallic origin, and are usually knitted up on a loom rather than on a circular knitting machine. The thickness of the yarn is indicated by its gauge, and this is indicated as 'gg'. A yarn for a hand-knit piece will have a low gauge of 3gg, whereas a very lightweight or fine gauge knit would be in 16-18gg. The number of the gauge refers to the number of rows to an inch, so the lower the number the thicker the yarn.

TIMINGS

The selection of the fabric begins when the concept is created. The designer will have some fabric ideas from the concept, which can be as vague as 'printed silk', or a 'textured wool'. At the same time as the developer is working with the sketches and the range plan, she is also working alongside the designer on the fabric selection. The designer has a clear idea about which fabrics should be used, but at this stage they are not yet finalised. Once the design process is underway, these ideas will start to become more specific, with a firmer view of the silk being a crepe, or the wool being a bouclé, and from there the selection goes one step deeper into different weights of fabric and different compositions that may be required. Maybe the silk will be a cotton silk mix, whereas the wool may be mixed with cashmere.

PLACES TO SELECT FABRICS

FABRIC FAIRS
Fabric fairs are the best places to source and select new fabrics and yarns, but what happens at the fairs, who works there and how does the fabric selection process work? Fabric mills show their collections at the fabric fairs twice a year, either directly or via agents, to designers, developers, and fabric buyers. Examples of some European fabric fairs are Première Vision (PV) in Paris, Munich Fabric Start in Germany or Milano Unica in Milan. But there are also many fairs in Asia and the USA. There is also a specific yarn fair in Florence.

FABRIC AGENTS
Agents are the middlemen between the fabric mill and the brand, with many being linked to more than one mill; they earn

Selecting fabrics at Première Vision in Paris.

their money from linking the right mill with the right customer. An advantage of using a fabric agent is that if they work with more than mill, you are able to see multiple collections in one appointment.

FABRIC MILLS

Fabric mills come in all shapes and sizes. Some are huge, covering many different types of fabrics (wools, linens, cottons and synthetics) and some specialise in one specific fabric type. Each mill will have a range relevant to the oncoming season, and their job is to entice the visitor into ordering a header card or colour card. The secrecy around the fabrics is due to the possibility of having fabric ideas stolen. The mills are very protective of their fabrics, and it is common for them not to allow you on their exhibition stand unless you have an appointment with the agent or with the mill directly.

Knitted strike offs and yarn dye panels ready for review and selection.

FABRIC DYEING

There are four main ways of buying fabric: as a yarn dye, piece dye, a printed fabric or greige. Understanding the differences will help you make informed fabric selections during the development stages.

YARN DYE

A yarn dye fabric is one which could be either a stripe, check or all over pattern, and whose colours are usually selected by the brand at yarn level. They will select colours from the yarn mill's colour card and will ask the fabric mill to make a hand loom for approval by the developer and the designer.

PIECE DYE

Piece dyed fabric is dyed after weaving, and is the most common of the techniques. The design team will either make a colour selection from the mill's colour card, or will submit its own shades for lab dipping.

PRINTED FABRIC

Some fabric mills have collections of fabric prints, which can be used as the header or recoloured to fit the brand's collection. It is also possible to have your own design printed by a fabric mill for something completely unique. In this case the mill will take the artwork from the brand, make a 'strike off' and send it to the designer or developer for approval. Once approved, the mill will weave up the fabric and send it to the garment factory.

GREIGE

Greige fabric is un-dyed, unfinished fabric, and is often ordered by brands when they are not yet in a position to select colours. They need to secure the fabric whilst the proto is being made in an available colour, but perhaps prefer to wait until the proto review to finalise shades. If they were to wait until the 1st garment review to book the fabric they might be too late. This is when greige is booked. Once the greige is booked, it undergoes a finishing process which makes it 'ready to dye' which makes it ready for either use in piece dye or garment dye.

GARMENT DYE

Garment dyeing is a method of fabric dyeing after it has been made into a garment. If a brand wants to have a garment that looks used or vintage, it will make the garment in a ready to dye fabric and submerge it in a vat of dye complete with its buttons, labels and thread. The whole garment comes out coloured if a little uneven in its shading. Brands, such as Pepe Jeans, and Abercrombie and Fitch, use garment dyes for some of their designs.

Fabric header cards.

Header card information

Mill name	ABC Mill	Article number	ABC123
Mill address	ABC House	Article name	Dusty
Contact details		Weight	150gm/m²
Email	info@abcfabric.com	Width	148 cm
		Composition	100% cotton

SELECTING FABRICS

If I'm selecting fabric for a designer or for a collection, I would make my research on the styles of garments the collection has, the price indications for the styles, and the ideas from the designer on the fabric types. I would draw up a short list of fabric mills and would make appointments to look at their collections to make selections against my list of requirements. From these selections I would order header cards.

SEASONAL CONSIDERATIONS

One point to make here is that depending on your final market (customer) you may need to have a good selection of all types and weights of fabrics. If you are based in Europe, but also sell to stores in Australia, you will need to incorporate a broader selection of fabric weights to accommodate the opposite seasons or climate. If it is a Spring range, the fabric weights will be lightweight, while in a Fall season the weights will be heavier (of course it is a little more complicated than that, but for the sake of simplicity let's keep it as this).

HEADER CARDS

This is a square of fabric (that can be up to 30cm x 30cm) with its technical details written on the top for reference. This will include the reference code for the fabric, the price, the colour reference number, the weight per m², the width and composition (100% wool, or 70% wool 30% cashmere, etc.). The designer orders headers like this from various mills to review them around 2 weeks later.

REVIEWING THE FABRICS

The review of the fabrics goes in three stages:

> **According to fabric type**
> Once I had received all the header cards from the mills I would split them up into fabric types, e.g. wool, silk, cotton, so that I had a clear spread of qualities.

> **According to construction and weight**
> From here I would subdivide the piles of header cards further into weave and weight, so all the satins, twills, bouclés, poplins, drills, denims, meltons, crepes and canvas were separate; this way I would have clearer comparison in order to make a better decision.

> **According to price**
> Finally, I would make a note of the price on top of each of the header cards; this is a very important factor in the decision making process, as the fabric price accounts for a high percentage of the cost price of the garment and has a major influence on the profit margin of the style.

MINIMUM ORDER CONSIDERATIONS

Every fabric mill has 'minimum order' quantities that it attaches to fabrics for sampling and also for production. The reason why minimums are set is as follows: to set up the machines to weave 1 m of the fabric is the same amount of effort as for 50 m, but there is more profit in 50 m than in 1 m. So, with this in mind the mill sets minimums accordingly. Sampling fabric is the term used for the quantity of fabric ordered for prototypes or salesman (selling samples). The minimums set by the fabric mills can either be per colour or per fabric article (this is an important fact to check at the fabric selection stage).

PER COLOUR

Fabric minimums per colour means you have to sell a lot of garments in one particular colour to meet fabric minimums, which is OK if the fabric is white, black or navy, but not so easy if it is yellow, pink or green. For instance, a men's shirt is made in green cotton poplin. The production minimums for this fabric are 500 m per colour. This means that you have to sell around 250 pieces of that shirt to meet the minimum order quantity. Depending on the shade of green, this could be easy or hard to achieve. It would be better if the minimums were around 100 m per colour, so that the brand would only have to sell around 50 pieces of the shirt to meet the minimums. A fabric with minimums of 500 m of a colour would not be a great choice in this example.

PER FABRIC ARTICLE

Fabric minimums per fabric article is much easier to work with for a brand, and this requirement means that it could be possible to have several colours of a fabric at lower quantities each and still be able to meet minimums. For instance, a wool bouclé fabric has production minimums of 1000 m per fabric. The fabric will be used for a jacket in four colours, which will equate to around 100 pieces of each jacket in each colour to reach the minimum. This is a great result, and it would be a great fabric for the developer to select and show the designer.

For sampling, where a small amount of fabric is needed for prototypes or for a set of salesman samples, the fabric minimum from the fabric mill is usually 50 m, but for production the quantities are much higher. In the production stage the fabric mills will quote anything from 100 to 1000 m minimums. There are, of course, exceptions depending on what size of fabric mill you

work with. The large mills in Asia, which are used to working with huge international companies, have very high minimum quantities and have less flexibility for smaller brands than the small Italian mills who have much more flexibility because they are used to working on smaller orders. The important point that needs to be understood is that most fabric mills will accommodate your sampling requests because they want to get production orders from you, as this is how they make their profit.

ALLOCATING FABRICS

The developer works closely with the designer to allocate the right fabrics to the designs, making sure that the weight, price and type of the fabric is both suitable for the garment's construction and is also in line with the designer's vision. Having a wide range of prices and styles of fabrics to choose from makes the allocation easier, but it is essential to understand what the designer wants from and for the garment.

THE RANGE PLAN AND ITS CONSEQUENCES TO FABRICS

The pyramid of basic, mid and top styles has already been introduced in the chapter on range planning, but for the sake of the fabric selection I will explain more about how the fabric prices affect the styles' position. Understanding where the style is in the pyramid will help you to select a fabric that is suitable for price.

FABRIC PRICING

Quite simply, if the style is a basic level shirt with a low retail selling price, the cost of the fabric needs to be low also, so that the brand will have a good profit margin. At the top of the pyramid there are the high fashion styles with a high retail price. These styles (although this is not imperative) can have a higher priced, more exclusive fabric, as they need to be visually rich and impressive enough to entice the consumer. The brand will still want to make profit on these styles, so it is not an excuse to go crazy at a fabric fair, but there is certainly some leeway allowed.

A selection of trade fairs for fabrics, prints, yarns and trends		
Bread & Butter	January and July	Breadandbutter.com
Expofil	February and September	Expofil.com
Magic	February and August	Magiconline.com
Milano Unica	February and September	Milanounica.it
Munich Fabric Start	January and September	Munichfabricstart.com
Pitti Immagine	January and July	Pittimmagine.com
Première Vision	February and September	Premierevision.com
Printsource New York	January, April and September	Printsourcenewyork.com

Allocating knit techniques and colours to sketches.

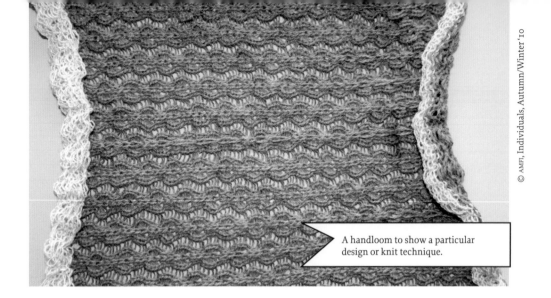

© AMFI, Individuals, Autumn/Winter '10

A handloom to show a particular design or knit technique.

ALLOCATING COLOUR

It has already been explained that colour is one of the four factors in the concept, and it is at this stage of the development process that the designer and the developer begin to consider the colours for each style and how the shades work with the proposed fabric selections.

STYLES AND OPTIONS

When allocating the colours to the fabrics, it is important to note that some of the styles will be made in more than one colour. The term for this is an 'option'. A style is a single item of clothing, such as a jacket or a skirt, and an option is a colour way, wash or finish of a style. So, for instance, if a jacket is made in three colours, it is one style in three options.

COLOUR CARDS

Most fabric mills and yarn suppliers have colour cards for their products, which the fabric mill collates for each fabric and yarn reference, and is based on trend predictions and their own history of sales. Some colours, such as black, navy, ivory and grey, sell consistently well season on

season, so these will always be on the shade card. Trend or seasonal colours, on the other hand, like yellow, green or pink would be seen as the 'seasonal' highlight colours of the fabric collection, and would be relevant for the season, but would be changed six months later. With the mills and the designers working from similar trends, their colour ideas often match. When the designer and developer begin the selecting colours, they try, wherever possible, to select from the mill's card, as this is a cheaper and quicker approach. If the desired colour is not available, the developer will ask the fabric mill to make a 'lab dip' of the brand's colour, but on the mill's fabric.

LAB DIPS

The process of lab dipping is more time consuming and more expensive, but ensures that the shade the designer selects remains consistent throughout the collection. It is a process that happens at both the development stage and production stage, whereby a colour lab (which works with the fabric mill) makes up the designer's shade in a chosen fabric by mixing a series of basic dyes. They then submit an offer to

A colourcard from a fabric mill.

the designer in three or more versions of the colour, including one that is closest to what the designer originally wanted. In some cases the designer will give some comments and direction to improve the colour. The lab notes these comments, the colour mixture is changed and new lab dips are submitted. This process continues until the designer gives the final approval.

HANDLOOMS

If the designer likes a fabric design but wants to change some of the colours of the weave, they request a 'handloom' to see before committing to the final fabric. A handloom is a small swatch of fabric made up on a handloom by the factory to show a particular design. It is also very common for designers to request their own handlooms from the fabric mill with their own designs. They may take colours from the fabric mill's colour card, but ask for a checked or striped fabric to the brand's design to be created. This makes the design more distinctive and tailored to the brand's own collection, but can be expensive for the mills.

FABRIC LEAD TIMES

The fabric for the salesman samples and for the production is the most time-sensitive issue in the whole process. On average, the lead times needed for fabrics to be made is 4-16 weeks; shorter if it is available in stock in the mill's warehouse; so, once the designer and the developer have considered the colour options and fabrics, it is crucial to make the fabric bookings.

FOR SAMPLING

With sampling the fabric lead times can be a little more flexible, with some of the fabric mills keeping small lengths of each fabric in stock to accommodate small orders or last minute requests. Small brands can often work well with this, but large brands may still have to wait for up to 4 weeks for sampling fabric. It is highly dependent on the mill and its location (Far Eastern mills take longer), so this is also an important thing to consider when selecting fabrics.

FOR PRODUCTION

Production orders take the longest time, and this is a major aspect of the planning process for the fabric mill and for the brand. With the timings of fabric weaving taking anything from 8 to 16 weeks, this is important information that needs to be communicated between the merchandise and the production teams to make sure they allow enough time for end garment delivery.

FABRIC ORDERING

Fabric orders are made at both the sampling and the production stage, and can be made either by the brand or by the factory. There are several different types of fabric orders that can be made when you have the sampling requirements or sales quantities from the designer or the sales teams. You can:

> **Book fabric per specific order;**
  (sampling or production)
> **Pre-book fabric;**
  (for a long lead time production fabric)
> **Or book stock fabric.**

PER ORDER
Booking per order is by far the simplest method of booking fabric. You have a sampling or production quantity, you know the fabric consumption needed to make all the garments and you send an order to the fabric mill. They respond with a fabric shipment date and this is relayed to the factory for their planning. It is a straightforward transaction.

FABRIC STOCK
Making a booking from stock fabric can be relevant in three different examples. The first example is in using greige fabric. The brand doesn't want to commit to a set of colours or fabric allocation right away, so they reserve a quantity of stock fabric, which the fabric mill will hold for a limited amount of time. Once the brand has decided on their style colour allocation, the mill will send it to the factory for sampling. For the second example, in the production capacity to book stock of a fabric means that it is booked to cover the sales order with some extra. Sometimes 25% extra is ordered to allow for the possibility of a reorder of the style. There is always a chance that this reorder is not placed, but to have 25% fabric left over is not too bad, and can be used for future proto samples. The third example is to use stock fabric for basic styles that run every season for a brand. In this case a quantity of fabric is held in stock and is called off by the factory every month to produce basic goods for a brand, which run throughout the season.

63

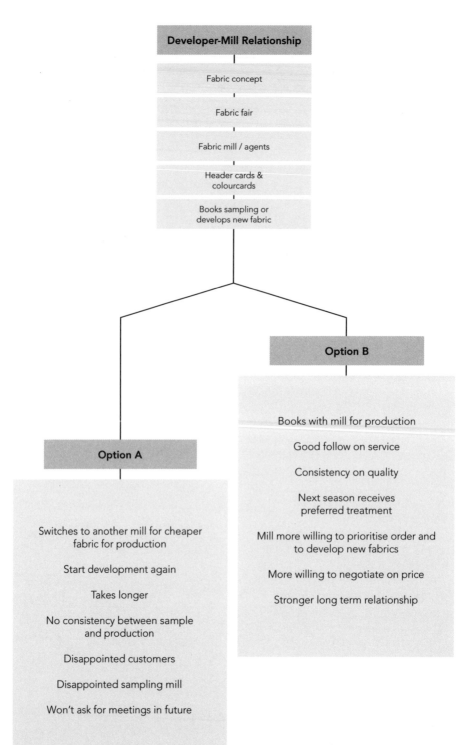

Developer-Mill Relationship

Fabric concept

Fabric fair

Fabric mill / agents

Header cards &
colourcards

Books sampling or
develops new fabric

Option B

Books with mill for production

Good follow on service

Consistency on quality

Next season receives
preferred treatment

Mill more willing to prioritise order and
to develop new fabrics

More willing to negotiate on price

Stronger long term relationship

Option A

Switches to another mill for cheaper
fabric for production

Start development again

Takes longer

No consistency between sample
and production

Disappointed customers

Disappointed sampling mill

Won't ask for meetings in future

PRE-BOOKING FABRIC

Fabric can be pre-booked at any point of the season; it ensures that production fabric is available whenever you want it. The risk involved in this is that the brand may be stuck with the fabric, which can be expensive if the intended style is cancelled and it is no longer required or no longer in the collection. Pre-booking needs to be managed carefully by the merchandise and production teams so that the brand isn't left with too much surplus fabric.

EXAMPLE

- -

A black cotton fabric has a lead-time of eight weeks and is needed in the factory in May. The final sales figures are given in February, so it is possible to order the fabric at the end of February and still have the fabric ready for the factories to begin sewing. However, a yarn dye fabric has a lead-time of twelve weeks and is also needed for the start of May. We know that the sales figures become available in February, but if we wait until they are finalised, we won't have the fabric available in time. At this stage we would pre-book the fabric at the end of January in order to have it ready when the factories need to start sewing. Pre-booking relies on forecast sales from the sales teams, and can result in an over stock of fabric if too much is bought, or an under stock if the sales figures turn out to be better than expected. This is the calculated risk taken by the merchandising team. Booking fabric only to cover a sales order is a safe way of booking fabric, but it means that you have no extra fabric available if the style becomes a best seller and you need to make a reorder. With fabric lead times of up to 8-16 weeks, a quick repeat order of a garment is not possible and sales are lost.

- -

This boucle tweed fabric may have high minimums and long leadtimes because of its construction complexity.

FABRIC BOOKING INFORMATION

What is important now is that the fabric is booked and that this process is in hand. With these pieces of information, you should be able to book fabric without any difficulty. A simple Excel form can be created with filters and then the relevant part sent to each mill to book fabric; it can also be used by development and production to track all changes throughout the process. It is a good idea to have one central file like this, with one person charged with keeping it up-to-date.

> **Fabric supplier** (mill name)
> **Fabric article code**
> **The factory the fabric will be allocated to**
> **Brand's colour name**
> **Mill's colour name**
  (this is very important. The brand may call a colour 'navy' but the mill may call it 265 on their colour card. It is very important that you follow the codes assigned by the fabric mill)
> **Fabric composition**
> **Price**
> **Lead-time**
> **Minimum order**

In a situation where the factory takes charge of the fabric booking, once the factory has the information on colour and order quantity from the brand's merchandise team, they start the fabric production process with the mills. The fabric team at the factory takes the order quantity of garments and with the consumption information (how much fabric is needed for one garment) calculates the amount of fabric needed for bulk. This is communicated to the fabric mill and they start weaving the fabric. It is very common for fabrics to be tested by the fabric mill for visual and dimensional changes in the production process.

SUBSTITUTING FABRIC

Sometimes the fabrics chosen for the garments need to be changed, cancelled or substituted by the developer or the production team. Reviews of the collection can raise questions of suitability to style or colour, and in production a low profit margin caused by using an expensive fabric can lead to a fabric substitution. Whatever the case, it is always best to work with the fabric mills from where the fabric came to see whether and how they can help.

AT SAMPLING

One of the reasons the developer and the designer review the prototypes is to check the fabric's suitability for the style. Sometimes a fabric is selected which, when the garment is made up, is seen not to be suitable for the particular style; perhaps the fabric is too heavy for the style, or maybe the fabric turns out to be not as the designer imagined. Whatever the case, the fabric will be changed. Remembering the matter of lead-times, the developer contacts the fabric mill or the manufacturing factory to see what they can suggest from their fabric stock. If the problem is with fabric weight, the developer will ask for a lighter or heavier version, if it is the whole look of the fabric, the developer will make alternative fabric suggestions to the designer, perhaps from fabrics they have already selected for other items or from their original fabric fair selection. Once an alternative is found, the factory and fabric mill are updated and the review continues.

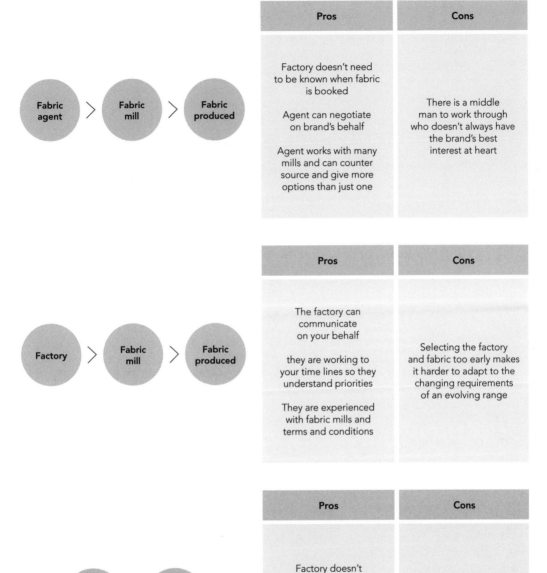

Pros	Cons
Factory doesn't need to be known when fabric is booked Agent can negotiate on brand's behalf Agent works with many mills and can counter source and give more options than just one	There is a middle man to work through who doesn't always have the brand's best interest at heart

Pros	Cons
The factory can communicate on your behalf they are working to your time lines so they understand priorities They are experienced with fabric mills and terms and conditions	Selecting the factory and fabric too early makes it harder to adapt to the changing requirements of an evolving range

Pros	Cons
Factory doesn't need to be known when the fabric is booked Brand has direct communication with mill Transparent relationship	Sometimes there is a language barrier which makes it hard to communicate

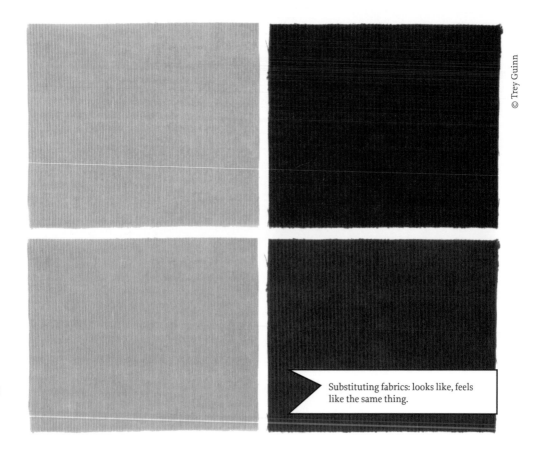

© Trey Guinn

Substituting fabrics: looks like, feels like the same thing.

AT PRODUCTION

In the production process the changes of fabric are more likely to be substitutions for a 'looks alike', 'feels alike' cheaper alternative. At this stage of the process, it is too late to completely change the fabric, as the garment has already been sold and there are orders next to it; so the production team will look, together with the original fabric mill, for an alternative fabric in, perhaps, a different blend or composition, but at a cheaper price. If something can be found at the original mill then a swap will be made and the production fabric booked. If the original mill cannot find an alternative, the production team will have to look further afield.

DENIM AND LEG PANELS

Until now I haven't singled out any fabrics specifically to focus on their unique properties, but denim is quite a specialised fabric, and the way it is treated in the development process is a little different from silk, wool or cotton. Denim, in general, is about fit, design, washing and finishing. There are thousands of things you can do with denim. You can keep it raw and unwashed, you can stonewash it, bleach it, add a rinse wash to it (to soften the hand feel), add a tint to it (to alter the colour shade), add abrasions to it (to give rips and tears), add a coating to it (to make it look like leather) or sandblast it, and the list goes on.

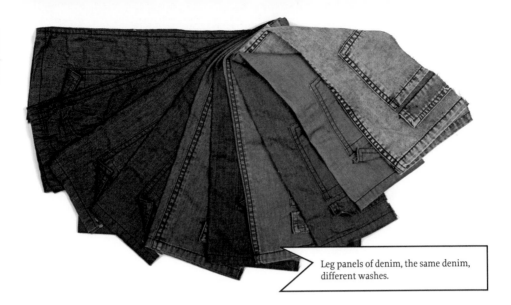

Leg panels of denim, the same denim, different washes.

It's also important to point out that denim is a fabric with many different weights (8oz, 10oz, 12oz, etc.) and constructions, all of which will react differently to the above treatments. A denim of 100% cotton could react very differently to a stone wash from a fabric of 98% cotton, 2% linen. There are hundreds of different combinations of finishes that can be achieved, and the best way to see these in proto form are either in a full pair of jeans or in a leg panel.

A leg panel is simply one leg of a pair of jeans that has a pocket (in some cases) and all the correct stitching methods, so that the end effect of the treatment can be properly seen. Compared to a flat piece of denim, you see more texture and a difference in colour – this is what needs to be approved, as this is more indicative of the end product. Naturally, it can't be fitted as it is only one leg, but it can still be approved for the final samples. Making leg panels of all the fabrics and treatments is a much quicker and cheaper alternative to full protos, thus making it a viable option for both factories and brands. It also ensures that you can see many leg panels, all with slight differences of washes or treatments.

It is not uncommon for a wash or finish to be made with different degrees of treatment, e.g. a rinse wash of 30 min or 45 min or 60 min or 90 min. Obviously, the longer the time the stronger the effect, so by seeing these on leg panels means that you can lay the panels out side by side and make easy comparisons – again aiding the decision making process. Once the leg panel has been approved, it is usually cut in half, with one piece kept at the brand's offices and the other at the factory. The factory will use this to replicate the wash and finish for the samples and later for production, and the brand will keep its half for the launch and also for later comparison at the production stage.

An additional point about leg panels is that their use isn't limited to just denim; sometimes brands use it for a chino fabric (cotton twill), which is available in many colour variations. Using leg panels to show the colour options is a great, time efficient process. Note to remember: leg panels are not just in denim.

FABRIC TESTING

All brands have specific testing requirements (usually set by the garment industry). The brand's production team instructs the factory and the fabric mill that the tests are needed and then monitors the testing procedure for the production process, so that the fabric can be produced correctly and to the brand's testing standards. Having the fabric tested helps to ensure a higher quality garment that will last longer for the consumer, and will add to the brand's quality reputation in the industry. One tip is to request a fabric test report at the fabric selection stage as this will avoid problems at a later stage when time is limited.

FABRIC TESTING REQUIREMENTS
Such tests include the following:

> **Flammability**
  (how does the fabric burn)
> **Dimensional change after dry**
  cleaning and washing (does it shrink)
> **Appearance after dry cleanings**
  (how does it look after it has
  been dry cleaned)
> **Spirality (twisting)**
> **Colour fastness to dry cleaning
  and washing** (does the colour run or
  bleed onto other fabrics)
> **Colour fastness to perspiration**
  (does the colour bleed or discolour)
> **Colour fastness to water**
> **Colour fastness to crocking** (rubbing)
> **Seam slippage**
> **Resistance to pilling** (the small balls
  that appear on woollen garments)

The failure of the pilling test has implications not only for the fabric, but also for the garment. If the wool fabric takes 8 weeks to manufacture, and it is discovered that it fails the resistance to pilling test, then there is a high chance that the fabric will need to be remade, adding an additional 8 weeks on the production schedule.

LATER STAGE FABRIC TESTING AND CHECKING
An additional element that needs to be added into the mix with some brands is that many companies use external fabric testing and checking facilities between the fabric mill and the factory to check the fabric's appearance, stability and width before it reaches the factory. The reason why a third party company is chosen to test the fabric is so that the results cannot be questioned by either the factory or the mill. This checking has both positive and negative implications for the following reasons. Usually, fabric production can take anything from 8 to 16 weeks. If the fabric needs to be sent from the mill to the 3rd party company, this can add an additional week. To check the fabric can take from three days to a week, depending on the order and the fabric type, and then if the results are good, it will take another week to reach the factory. So, we have an additional three weeks minimum to the production time, which, of course, needs to be planned by the factory. Below are some fabric issues identified in bulk fabric checking, and their implications.

SELVEDGE SHADING
The selvedges of the fabric are the edges (sides). Selvedge shading is when there are different shades of colour from the edge of the fabric to the centre of the tested piece. Using a fabric that is not of a uniform colour means that some parts of the garment will

TRUE STORY

I worked for a brand that had a tightly woven wool fabric for a winter skirt. The pilling result for the fabric was too low which meant that the amount of small balls that appeared on the fabric was too high when it was tested using a 3rd party centre. As you can imagine, to have this result on a skirt that has high friction areas is not acceptable so we approached the fabric mill to ask what they could do to improve the result. The factory accepted the fabric back and then reconditioned it by shearing the surface slightly to remove some of the surface hair and that improved the result for the brand to accept.

In this case the solution was workable but if the fabric had been a looser weave then to shear the surface would have made the base threads more visible and weaker for construction, so making it unstable to use (the garments would fall apart). Not every test works for every fabric, so we are reliant on the skills of the fabric mill and the testing centre to recommend the best course of action.

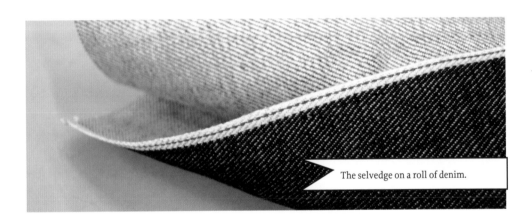

The selvedge on a roll of denim.

be different in colour from the rest. Imagine having a navy trench coat where the sleeves looked a lighter colour than the body.

CREASES
Sometimes the fabric is creased throughout the rolls. In most cases the fabric can be pressed and then used without problems, but if the fabric is a corduroy or a velvet and the nap of the fabric is damaged, it can't be used and the fabric has to be remade.

USEABLE WIDTH
Most fabric has a standard width depending on the fabric looms it was made on, but when the actual width is less than what has been agreed, this has implications on how the pattern pieces can be laid out, which in turn affects the number of garments that can be made from a given length.

It should be the mill's responsibility to ensure that all these issues are addressed

Bureau Veritas Hong Kong Limited

PRICING INFORMATION
價格資料
MANDATORY TEST

Woven Fabric (Core test items)
Package Price (net)

List of Test Items included
1. Color Fastness to Laundering or Dry Cleaning (Accelerated)
2. Color Fastness to Crocking
3. Color Fastness to Light
4. Colorfastness to Non-Chlorine Bleach
5. Flammability (Non-exempt fabrics only, All colors)

Denim Fabric (Core test items)
Package Price (net)

t of Test Items included
1. Color Fastness to Laundering or Dry Cleaning (Accelerated)
2. Color Fastness to Crocking
Colorfastness to Light
H Value (Washed Garment, Washed Denim & white)

ore test items)

		Hong Kong	
USD 41		HKD	322

Test Method
AATCC 61
AATCC 8 & 116
AATCC/ASTM 16 / D...
16 CFR 1610

USD 52   Hong Kong   HKD

before the fabric leaves the mill, so that the fabric can be approved and sent to the factory without problems. If, however, there are problems, it is the brand's responsibility to make a decision on the action taken.

FABRIC TESTING COMPANIES

Usually, when the fabric mill develops a fabric, all these tests are carried out in the early stages, so there is already a set of test results on hand. However, all fabric needs to be tested to ensure that the fabric passes either to industry standards or to the brand's own standards. Most brands have accredited testing companies where the fabrics can be sent. Under no circumstances will a brand accept another testing company's results, as they can be connected to the fabric mill and this can have bias implications on the tests.

Intertek and SGS are two companies who work internationally with brands to ensure that the fabrics, fibers and yarns meet industry requirements. If you are in the position of being able to visit one of these testing centers, you should do so, as the insight into fabric production is fascinating, and it gives a fuller picture of the issues and implications. This knowledge can be used at the initial selection stage to prevent later problems. For example, having an indication of the pilling test result available when selecting the fabric can eliminate later problems in production. If the mill knows that one fabric is borderline pass/fail for pilling, whereas a similar one with a different composition passes easily, then pick the one that has passed.

- -

Learn the basics on fabric types and construction,
as this will give you a good grounding.

Fabric mills and agents love to talk about fabrics.
For them it is their passion and for you this is a free
education. Listen and learn, as their knowledge
comes from years of experience.

When I meet with a fabric supplier the first things
I ask are; what is the fabric weight, weave and
composition? How much is it? What are the minimums?
What is the lead time? This is a good starting point
for any fabric appointment.

Understand how colour works with fabric. Not
every colour will work with every fabric type.

The subject of fabrics is huge. There is always
something new to learn. Read the industry press to
keep up-to-date on fabric price concerns or new
developments.

- -

V

Chapter 5: **Development and Production Information Flow**

The creation, design, development and production of a collection involve the generation, sharing and distribution of a huge amount of information. The information flow from the start of the development process to the end of production is a crucial element for the successful internal workings of the brand and for the external relationships with the factories, trim suppliers and customers.

For some companies the initial basis of all information is a development matrix, which is created at the start of the design process to catalogue all the styles, fabric details and colours; this is managed by the development team, and some of the information is shared with factories. Another method of collating this information is via a PLM (product lifecycle management) system, which is a software package, which, once the basic data has been entered for each style, tracks the data and changes just as the development matrix or technical pack does. Details of these systems can be found in the list of useful websites at the end of the book (p. 227).

Once the collection is ready to launch, the development matrix is merged into the line list, which is a financially driven document based on the original matrix, but used by the sales and merchandising teams. Within a few weeks this document is adjusted again to take into consideration the production planning. The production team adapts the line list, adding key date information, which is shared with the factories. This one document at the start of the creation of the collection can drive the flow of information until the final goods have been shipped from the factory.

During the development, sales and production stages information is changing hourly, so it is vital to update the documents and keep the information current. A style that has been designed but not entered in the development matrix may not be sent to a factory, so the proto will not be made. An incorrect cost price in the line list at the collection launch will equate to an incorrect

MATRIX	A	SPRING SEASON										
RANGE	DEL DROPS	VENDOR	C/O	#	PRODUCT GROUP	HANGING	W/M	PROTO NUMBER	TOTAL SAMPLE REQ	STYLE NAME/DESCRIPTION	COLOUR	FABRIC
NEW BRAND	1 ONLY	AMAZING SHIRTS	EU	1	SHIRTS	FLAT	M	M4A002	5	ANDREW LS SHIRT	WHITE	BASIC POPLIN
NEW BRAND	1 ONLY	AMAZING SHIRTS	EU		SHIRTS	FLAT	M	M4A002	5	ANDREW LS SHIRT	BLACK	BASIC POPLIN
NEW BRAND	1 ONLY	AMAZING SHIRTS	EU		SHIRTS	FLAT	M	M4A002	5	ANDREW LS SHIRT	NAVY	BASIC POPLIN
NEW BRAND	1 ONLY	AMAZING SHIRTS	EU	1	SHIRTS	FLAT	M	M4A004	5	BOB SLIM FIT LS SHIRT	WHITE	STRETCH POPLIN
NEW BRAND	1 ONLY	AMAZING SHIRTS	EU		SHIRTS	FLAT	M	M4A004	5	BOB SLIM FIT LS SHIRT	BLACK	STRETCH POPLIN
NEW BRAND	1 ONLY	CRAFTED SHIRTS	EU	1	SHIRTS	FLAT	M	M4A006A	5	CHARLIE S SLV SHIRT	GREEN	POPLIN STRIPE
NEW BRAND	1 ONLY	CRAFTED SHIRTS	EU	1	SHIRTS	FLAT	M	M4A006B	5	CHARLIE S SLV SHIRT	GREEN	POPLIN STRIPE
NEW BRAND	1 ONLY	FANCY SHIRTS	FE	1	SHIRTS	FLAT	M	M4A008	5	DAVID SLIM FIT S SLVE SHIRT	WHITE	STRETCH POPLIN
NEW BRAND	1 ONLY	FANCY SHIRTS	FE	1	SHIRTS	FLAT	M	M4A010	5	EDDIE SLIM FIT FANCY CUFF SHIRT	BLACK	STRETCH POPLIN
NEW BRAND	1 ONLY	AMAZING SHIRTS	EU	1	SHIRTS	FLAT	M	M4A012A	5	CHARLIE S SLV SHIRT	WHITE	BASIC POPLIN
NEW BRAND	1 ONLY	CRAFTED SHIRTS	EU	1	SHIRTS	FLAT	M	M4A012B	5	CHARLIE S SLV SHIRT	WHITE	BASIC POPLIN
NEW BRAND	1 ONLY	AMAZING SHIRTS	EU	1	SHIRTS	FLAT	M	M4A014	5	FRANK LS SLV BUTTON DOWN SLIM	WHITE	STRETCH POPLIN
NEW BRAND	1 ONLY	AMAZING SHIRTS	EU	1	SHIRTS	FLAT	M	M4A014	5	FRANK LS SLV BUTTON DOWN SLIM	NAVY	STRETCH POPLIN
NEW BRAND	1 ONLY	FANCY SHIRTS	FE	1	SHIRTS	FLAT	M	M4A016	5	GRAHAM LS SLV BUTTON DOWN	GREEN	CHECK POPLIN
NEW BRAND	1 ONLY	AMAZING SHIRTS	EU	1	SHIRTS	FLAT	M	M4A018	5	HARRY SLSV EPAULETTE SHIRT	BLACK	BASIC POPLIN
NEW BRAND	1 ONLY	FANCY SHIRTS	FE	1	SHIRTS	FLAT	M	M4A020	5	IAN SSLV SHIRT	BLUE	CHECK POPLIN
NEW BRAND	1 ONLY	FANCY SHIRTS	FE	1	SHIRTS	FLAT	M	M4A022	5	JOHN PLEAT FRONT SHIRT	WHITE	STRETCH POPLIN
NEW BRAND	1 ONLY	AMAZING SHIRTS	EU	1	SHIRTS	FLAT	M	M4A024	5	KEITH LS SHIRT	RED	POPLIN STRIPE

FABRIC CODE	FABRIC DETAILS	PRICE CODE	TARGET PRICE Eur	RRP	FACTORY PROTO PRICE	OPTION COUNT	GWS SENT	PROTO RECEIVED	PROTO APPRD	2ND PROTO NEEDED	2ND PROTO RECEIVED	2ND PROTO APPRD
ABC 122# 1	100% COTTON	BASIC				1	24TH FEB	12TH APRIL				
ABC 122# 1	100% COTTON	BASIC				1	24TH FEB	12TH APRIL				
ABC 122# 1	100% COTTON	BASIC				1	24TH FEB	12TH APRIL				
STRETCH 8YU-1	98% COTTON 2 % ELASTANE	BASIC				1	24TH FEB	12TH APRIL				
STRETCH 8YU-1	98% COTTON 2 % ELASTANE	BASIC				1	24TH FEB	12TH APRIL				
PINSTRIPE 5-4	97% COTTON 3 % POLYESTER	BASIC				1	24TH FEB	12TH APRIL				
PINSTRIPE 5-4	97% COTTON 3 % POLYESTER	BASIC				1	24TH FEB	12TH APRIL				
STRETCH 8YU-1	98% COTTON 2 % ELASTANE	MID				1	15TH FEB	5TH APRIL				
STRETCH 8YU-1	98% COTTON 2 % ELASTANE	MID				1	15TH FEB	5TH APRIL				
ABC 122# 1	100% COTTON	MID				1	24TH FEB	12TH APRIL				
ABC 122# 1	100% COTTON	MID				1	24TH FEB	12TH APRIL				
STRETCH 8YU-1	98% COTTON 2 % ELASTANE	MID				1	24TH FEB	12TH APRIL				
STRETCH 8YU-1	98% COTTON 2 % ELASTANE	MID				1	15TH FEB	5TH APRIL				
BRAVO CHECK 121A	100% COTTON	TOP				1	24TH FEB	12TH APRIL				
ABC 122# 1	100% COTTON	TOP				1	15TH FEB	5TH APRIL				
BRAVO CHECK 121A	100% COTTON	TOP				1	24TH FEB	12TH APRIL				
STRETCH 8YU-1	98% COTTON 2 % ELASTANE	TOP				1	15TH FEB	5TH APRIL				
PINSTRIPE 5-4	97% COTTON 3 % POLYESTER	TOP				1	24TH FEB	12TH APRIL				

profit margin and could cause a cancellation; an incorrect shipment date in the production schedule can mean a late delivery for a factory. It is extremely important to have a clear flow of information and dedicated people to keep it updated.

THE DEVELOPMENT MATRIX

The development matrix is the starting point for the flow of information for the whole collection; it is an Excel chart, which holds the majority of the details of the tech packs for the range being developed. It can also be known as the style list /product list or style bible. Whatever the name, it is an extremely important document and without it the whole development process would be a mess of epic proportions.

Even the most organised of individuals gets confused throughout the development process, as there are daily changes to styles, fabrics, colours and dates. It is essential to have one form and, if possible, one person with the responsibility to update it.

WHO CREATES IT?

The development matrix is created by a member of the development team as the design team sketches. It should be ready to be compiled as the sketches are handed to the developer. With the matrix being a working document, it is important that the one person who adds, cancels and changes the style information doesn't delete anything. It is crucial for the development team that every style remains visible on the matrix even if it has been cancelled. Styles can be reinstated and recancelled; so, by using a simple colour-coding system it is easy to see the current style status. I usually colour the cells grey for a cancelled style and yellow if I have made a change to it. Choose your own colour-coding, but make sure everyone in your team understands it, so that they can read it accurately.

WHEN IS IT USED?

If the matrix is filled in correctly with the factory name, it is possible to filter the document and send the factory a copy of the section relating to their styles. This is a great cross checking method, and one that I use all the time. It also means that the factory can use your information system, which is helpful when requesting progress updates from them on the status of samples.

KEY ELEMENTS

Key elements to include are:

> **Prototype number** (used for identifying the garment throughout the process)
> **Vendor / factory**
> **Product group**
> **Style quantity**
> **Style name and description**
> **Colour**
> **Fabric**
> **Fabric reference code**
> **Price code** (basic, mid or top target price)
> **Hanging or flat**
  (how the goods will be delivered to the stores, either on hangers or folded)
> **Number of samples required**
  (this is for the selling process)

The development matrix is the single most important document that a developer can work with, and should be treated accordingly. As soon as the style is designed, it should be entered into the file and a proto number allocated. Other aspects, like fabric and

colour, can be added as they are confirmed between the developer and designer, but it is crucial to enter every style as soon as it is handed to the developer. There will be times when you have to change the matrix 30 times in a day, but do so as the changes occur and you will always know what the development situation is.

PROTO NUMBERS

A proto number is a unique number linked to a designers sketch. They are constructed in a specific way so that they are unique to the

Proto numbers	
Mens	M
Womens	W
Kids	K
Season	
Fall	1
Holiday	2
Pre spring	3
Spring	4
Summer	5
Pre fall	6
Product group	
Shirts	A
Pants	B
Jackets	C
Jersey	D
Sweater knits	E
Accessories	F
etc.	
Unique number	
Men	Odd
Women	Even
For example:	
fall mens shirt = M1A003	

style, season, and product group. The number will stay with the style throughout the whole process and is used by the factories as a way of identifying the style. Here is one method of creating the numbers:

STYLE NAME AND DESCRIPTION

The style name and description stays with the garment right through to the shop floor. To add a name and the description to the style allows everyone from developer to sales person at the end stage to sell an object and to have a connection with it. The style name and description may seem like an unnecessary use of time and energy; after all, there is already a proto number to describe the garment, but remember that this is a creative process, a number is a logical and analytical way to code a garment, but it doesn't give details on the fit, fabric or styling. For example, which of the following gives you more instant and comprehensible information about a shirt: Jonathan Long Sleeve shirt with button down collar and bias cut pocket or the code number M4A003?

Trying to invent a new set of names each season is a long process. Some brands pick a theme each season and then find appropriate names to match. First names, city names or names of flowers have been used in the past. If the concept of your range is rock and roll, then search for names of rock bands or musicians. At one time when I worked for a brand, one season we named our men's range after foods. Each product group had a different country; outerwear was Italian, woven tops was French and sweaters was Indian. We had a Basmati V neck and a Pesto down-filled jacket. In most companies a style will have a name and a proto number.

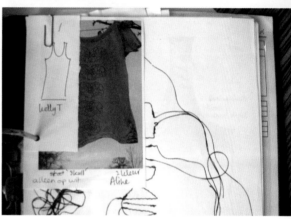

THE TECHNICAL PACK

The technical pack, also known as tech pack, BOM (bill of materials) or GWS (garment work sheet), is a document produced by the development team informing the factory of all the details relating to the style; it should correspond exactly to the development matrix, but have much more detail in its content. The factory will take the information in the pack and make an initial prototype of the style that will then be reviewed by the brand. Tech packs are time consuming to update, but if the pack is complete from the start of the process, it remains a solid reference point. My advice is, never skimp on information and never assume that the people at the factory know

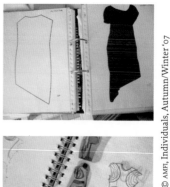
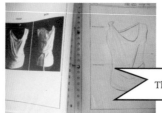

The different pages of a technical pack.

80

what you mean. Give too much information rather than too little, and always make sure that the information in the technical pack matches all the additional information handed over (like pattern, sketch and spec).

Updating the tech packs is a regular occurrence, especially when they are being created. Ideas change, labels are added and buttons removed, so it is very much a working document. As with the development matrix, it helps to maintain consistency if one developer updates the same tech packs. This is not to say that the developer manages the whole range, but splitting up the collection between team members means that each person has sole responsibility for their section and they update their own styles accordingly. Once the technical packs have been created, it is quite normal to ask colleagues in the development team to read them over before they are sent out to get a fresh pair of eyes on the product. It is too easy to assume that everything is clear, when you have been staring at it for days at a time.

KEY PAGES
Key pages are:

> **Front page** (the sketch, proto number, style name and fabric details)
> **Technical page** (detailed sketch with additional technical details to note)
> **Size specification sheet** (tracks all the measurements and changes throughout process)
> **Fabric and trim detail/BOM** (details on all fabrics, buttons, branding and stitching)
> **Label details** (label codes, colours and positions)
> **Proto comment** (comments and details about proto fittings)
> **Selling sample** (sales sample) comment (comments at the next stage)
> **Pre-production comments** (production comments)
> **Graded spec** (used in production)

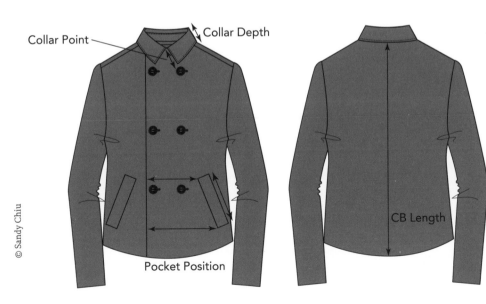

Collar Point

Collar Depth

Pocket Position

CB Length

The fact that one document can follow the process from start to finish (like the development matrix) means that you have a full history to refer to not only for the current season, but also in future seasons, if a style is to be revisited and updated. For the majority of the pages the developer works with the designer to ensure that all the details relating to fabric, colour and look are workable. In general, at the very early stages of building the range the designer works with the developers, and together they determine the 'fits' or 'blocks' of the garments, and the pattern makers realize those fits and create the patterns or base patterns.

WHO CREATES IT?

The developer creates the tech pack once she has received the sketches from the designer. One of the most complicated aspects of the tech pack is the size specification. I have already mentioned that the designer and the developer discuss the 'fit' of the style, but the pattern creation by the pattern maker is something that takes time and skill.

THE PATTERN MAKER

The pattern maker is a technically trained designer who can create patterns from sketches. They can work for the brand or for the factory, and can turn the sketch of the

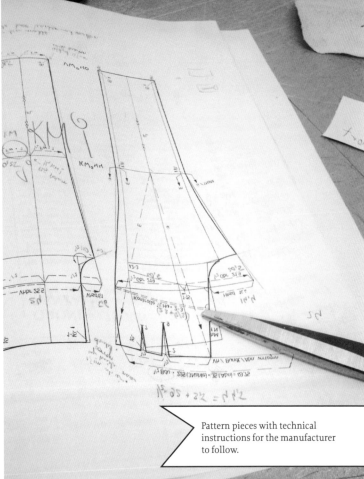

Pattern pieces with technical
instructions for the manufacturer
to follow.

designer into an actual garment by applying
the base measurements and calculations.

FIT OR BLOCK

A 'fit' is a description to explain the
silhouette of a garment. A 'block' is a basic
pattern, which is made with the specific
customer measurements for the brand.
Blocks come first, then arrives the fit.
Sometimes blocks are not used at all and a
new fit is made from scratch. The designer
gives the developer a silhouette or fit with
the sketch, and it is then up to the developer
to create the size spec with the assistance of
the pattern maker. These 'fits' refer to a set

of measurements, which can make the shirt
tight or loose. These measurements are
carefully constructed by the pattern maker
to ensure that the proportions of the garment
are correct and that the fit is appropriate for
the market (the end customer).

Each brand has a target customer they
sell to and each customer has a specific fit.
The Japanese market in general uses smaller
proportions than do most Europeans. The
German market has much bigger proportions
than those of the Spanish market. So, what
this means is that if a company is supplying
to the Far East as well as Northern Europe,

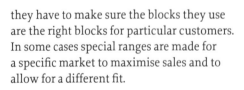
Making a paper pattern.

they have to make sure the blocks they use are the right blocks for particular customers. In some cases special ranges are made for a specific market to maximise sales and to allow for a different fit.

BASE MEASUREMENTS
The base measurements are the starting point from which the size spec of the style can be generated. From this point, pockets can be created, the collar made bigger, the hips made wider or the sleeve made shorter. Creating base measurements takes time, but it is time well spent, as it gives a strong identity to the brand, and reassurance to the customer that the fit of their garment will be the same next time they buy it. Without the base measurements there will

be no standardisation in fits, which means a confused customer who may not remain a customer for long. Some of the best brands have the same fits every season, but in different colours or fabrics. This makes it much easier to keep the customers happy, as they immediately know the fit and will buy replacement garments season on season. An example of this is the Levi 501.

SIZE SPEC
A size spec is the collective group of measurements derived from the fit or block for the chest, length, waist, hip, armhole, collar, etc. Everything needed to make the paper pattern for the garment is included, and is followed by the pattern maker or the factory.

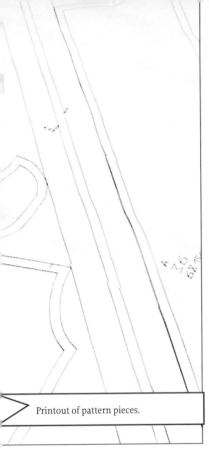

Printout of pattern pieces.

Making a toile on a tailoring dummy.

MAKING PATTERNS

With the fit selected, the pattern maker and developer can work their magic and create the designer's vision. Depending on the pattern maker and the facilities available, they will work either by hand, making the pattern first on paper and then on card, or digitally with a specialised computer program, which allows the maker to 'plot' or mark key points of the pattern on a digital device, which transfers it on to paper, which can then be printed out and checked. Of course, there is often a combination of the two, but it depends on what the garment is, the complexity of the style and the skill of the maker.

TOILE

Once completed, the paper pattern is sent to the factory and sometimes a toile is made as a test. A toile is a version of a garment made by the factory to test a pattern, and is usually made in a simple cotton or other cheap fabric. Sometimes this is done for complicated garments, or in some cases a section of the garment (maybe a collar or an unusual sleeve shape) is made to see the proportions or fit. The toile is fitted by the pattern maker and then the comments are sent back to the factory for the proto sample to be completed. From this pattern they can also advise what the actual measurements can be (how long the sleeve is, how tight the waist is, etc.; is there a collar? If so, is it a pointy one or a round one?). Not every

Handing over tech packs to
a manufacturer.

TRUE STORY

I worked for a brand once and the designer wanted to have a pair of jeans developed with a specific wash, branding and pocket detail. We sent the tech pack off to the factory with instructions, along with reference pants that we had taken from a previous season collection with some added updates and features.

We received the prototype a few weeks later and on the leg of the jeans was a mark of a ring, around 3 inches wide and in a pale brown colour. We had absolutely no idea what this mark was from, and clearly, it was not what we wanted, so we checked with the factory as to why they had made the sample with a brown circle on the leg.

By return, they sent is a picture of the sample that we had sent them. On the leg was the ring mark from a cup of coffee that has been sitting on the pants. It was interpreted by the factory that this was a 'design feature' and that it was what we had requested. Here is an example of why it is good to handover in person.

design development team has a pattern maker, but they are crucial to the long-term fit of the garments. In some cases the toile is made in house to save time and to see immediate results. This also makes it less complicated for the factory as they receive just one final pattern and not various versions of the same pattern.

HANDOVER TO FACTORIES

Handovers happen regularly for the development and production teams, from the initial tech pack handover, the proto review, the second proto review and at production and pre production. A handover of the styles can be done in two ways. The first is either via email or courier, which means sending the packs off to the factory and waiting for them to read and digest the information. The second alternative, which is by far the best, is for the developer and

the designer to go to the factory personally and spend a few days working through the tech packs with the people there. In these meetings there is a team of people: factory managers, fabric managers and pattern makers discussing each style, the fit, the fabric, the linings, the technical issues, everything that is involved. In either scenario, questions are always raised about the styles' details, but if the developer and the designer are at the factory, face to face with their team, the process of resolving problems and answering questions is quick and painless.

THE LINE LIST

Once all the proto reviews are completed and the final salesman samples are being made, the development team completes the development matrix with all colours,

	A	B	C	D	E	F	G	H	I	J	K	L
LINELIST		**C**			**SPRING SEASON**							
	RANGE	DEL DROPS	VENDOR	C/O	#	PRODUCT GROUP	HANGING	W/M	PROTO NUMBER	TOTAL SAMPLE REQ	STYLE NAME/DESCRIPTION	COLOUR
	NEW BRAND	1 ONLY	AMAZING SHIRTS	EU	1	SHIRTS	FLAT	M	M4A002	5	ANDREW LS SHIRT	WHITE
	NEW BRAND	1 ONLY	AMAZING SHIRTS	EU		SHIRTS	FLAT	M	M4A002	5	ANDREW LS SHIRT	NAVY
	NEW BRAND	1 ONLY	AMAZING SHIRTS	EU	1	SHIRTS	FLAT	M	M4A004	5	BOB SLIM FIT LS SHIRT	WHITE
	NEW BRAND	1 ONLY	AMAZING SHIRTS	EU		SHIRTS	FLAT	M	M4A004	5	BOB SLIM FIT LS SHIRT	BLACK
	NEW BRAND	1 ONLY	AMAZING SHIRTS	EU	1	SHIRTS	FLAT	M	M4A006A	5	CHARLIE S SLV SHIRT	GREEN
	NEW BRAND	1 ONLY	CRAFTED SHIRTS	EU		SHIRTS	FLAT	M	M4A006B	5	CHARLIE S SLV SHIRT	GREEN
	NEW BRAND	1 ONLY	FANCY SHIRTS	FE	1	SHIRTS	FLAT	M	M4A010	5	EDDIE SLIM FIT FANCY CUFF SHIRT	BLACK
	NEW BRAND	1 ONLY	FANCY SHIRTS	FE		SHIRTS	FLAT	M	M4A010	5	EDDIE SLIM FIT FANCY CUFF SHIRT	WHITE
	NEW BRAND	1 ONLY	AMAZING SHIRTS	EU	1	SHIRTS	FLAT	M	M4A012A	5	CHARLIE S SLV SHIRT	WHITE
	NEW BRAND	1 ONLY	CRAFTED SHIRTS	EU	1	SHIRTS	FLAT	M	M4A012B	5	CHARLIE S SLV SHIRT	WHITE
	NEW BRAND	1 ONLY	AMAZING SHIRTS	EU	1	SHIRTS	FLAT	M	M4A014	5	FRANK LS SLV BUTTON DOWN SLIM	WHITE
	NEW BRAND	1 ONLY	AMAZING SHIRTS	EU		SHIRTS	FLAT	M	M4A014	5	FRANK LS SLV BUTTON DOWN SLIM	NAVY
	NEW BRAND	1 ONLY	FANCY SHIRTS	FE	1	SHIRTS	FLAT	M	M4A016	5	GRAHAM LS SLV BUTTON DOWN	GREEN
	NEW BRAND	1 ONLY	AMAZING SHIRTS	EU	1	SHIRTS	FLAT	M	M4A018	5	HARRY SLSV EPAULETTE SLIM FIT SHIRT	BLACK
	NEW BRAND	1 ONLY	FANCY SHIRTS	FE	1	SHIRTS	FLAT	M	M4A020	5	IAN SSLV SHIRT	BLUE
	NEW BRAND	1 ONLY	FANCY SHIRTS	FE	1	SHIRTS	FLAT	M	M4A022	5	JOHN PLEAT FRONT SHIRT	WHITE
	NEW BRAND	1 ONLY	AMAZING SHIRTS	EU	1	SHIRTS	FLAT	M	M4A024	5	KEITH LS SHIRT	RED

	P	Q	R	S	T	U	AD	AE	AF	AG	AH	AI	AJ	AK	AL
			RRP/6.4	CPX2	T X SAMPL#										
	PRICE CODE	RRP	APPX CP	PROTO DEV COST	TOTAL SAMPLE COST	OPTION COUNT	COST PRICE	WHOLESALE PRICE	LANDED PRICE	RRP	MARGIN	WEIGHTED MARGIN	BUY QUANTITY	EX SOURCE DEL DATE	PURCHASE ORDER NUMBER
	BASIC	100,00	15,63	31,25	156,25	1	15,63	40,00	18,44	100,00	53,9		250	Nov	123543
	BASIC	100,00	15,63	31,25	156,25	1							300		
	BASIC	100,00	15,63	31,25	156,25	1							500		
	BASIC	100,00	15,63	31,25	156,25	1							400		
	BASIC		0,00	0,00	0,00	1									
	BASIC	100,00	15,63	31,25	156,25	1							300		
	MID	120,00	18,75	37,50	187,50	1							150		
	MID	120,00	18,75	37,50	187,50	1							300		
	MID		0,00	0,00	0,00	1									
	MID	120,00	18,75	37,50	187,50	1							300		
	MID	120,00	18,75	37,50	187,50	1							220		
	MID	120,00	18,75	37,50	187,50	1							200		
	MID	120,00	18,75	37,50	187,50	1							150		
	TOP		0,00	0,00	0,00	1									
	TOP	130,00	20,31	40,63	203,13	1							200		
	TOP	130,00	20,31	40,63	203,13	1							200		
	TOP	130,00	20,31	40,63	203,13	1							100		

correct fabrics, cost prices and style names, ready for the merchandise team to take over. They take the spreadsheet just before the collection is launched and begin adding business reporting codes, and price and profit margin calculations to transform the information sheet into its next stage. This is the point when it turns into the line list.

This document is now the key tool for all style information, and is used extensively by the merchandising team for sales. The Excel document should be rich in detail necessary for the selling of the garments and the financial reporting for the brand.

KEY ELEMENTS

The document can take many guises for different companies, but the essential information should be as set out below. As with the development matrix, some software systems can set up a detailed line list for you, but at the same time, an Excel file can also work. If you start with the information from the development matrix, you can build a line list from there. It can be as simple or as complicated as you require:

> **Style information**
> **Fabric**
> **Colour**
> **RRP** (Recommended Retail Price)
> **Cost price**
> **Wholesale price**
> **Landed price**
> **Margin**
> **Weighted margin**
> **Buy quantity**
> **Ex source date**
> **Size offer**
> **Purchase order number**

WHO CREATES IT?

The line list is created by the merchandise team just before the launch, and is used as a working document throughout the preparation of sales and sales period. As with the development matrix, it is preferable that one person updates the list as necessary, to ensure that the information is entered consistently and accurately. It is used to collate the financial information for the collection from profit margins and order quantities to unconfirmed ex factory shipment dates.

WHEN IS IT USED?

The line-list is used throughout the time period of pre launch to post sales and purchase order creation. It is also used for sales analysis for the next season, once the current collection has been shipped.

PRODUCTION PLANNING

Production planning is the final stage of the information flow, and is managed jointly between the factory and the brand's production team. Many brands have their own production planning sheets that they share with their vendor, so the information they receive from all factories is consistent in format and can be collated into one file. There is one key date that the factory and brand need to maintain, and that is the bulk shipping date, but with so many individual processes having to be carried out between the receipt of the purchase order and ex shipment date, it is for the timely conduct of these that the production planning is essential. The sheet can be created with information retrieved from the line list and is then expanded with some additional columns.

SPRING PRODUCTION PLANNING — E

Vendor	Purch.Do	Curr.ESD	Colou	Material description	Fabric	Sum of Quantit
AMAZING SHIRTS	123543	15TH NOV	WHITE	ANDREW LS SHIRT	BASIC POPLIN	250
AMAZING SHIRTS	123543	15TH NOV	NAVY	ANDREW LS SHIRT	BASIC POPLIN	300
AMAZING SHIRTS	145821	15TH DEC	WHITE	BOB SLIM FIT LS SHIRT	STRETCH POPLIN	500
AMAZING SHIRTS	145821	15TH DEC	BLACK	BOB SLIM FIT LS SHIRT	STRETCH POPLIN	400
CRAFTED SHIRTS	147890	15TH NOV	GREEN	ANDREW LS SHIRT	POPLIN STRIPE	250
FANCY SHIRTS	148654	15TH NOV	BLACK	EDDI SLIM FIT FANCY CUFF SHIRT	STRETCH POPLIN	150
FANCY SHIRTS	148654	15TH NOV	WHITE	EDDI SLIM FIT FANCY CUFF SHIRT	STRETCH POPLIN	300
CRAFTED SHIRTS	150222	15TH JAN	WHITE	CHARLIE S SLV SHIRT	BASIC POPLIN	300
AMAZING SHIRTS	151234	15TH DEC	WHITE	FRANK LS SLV BUTTON DOWN SHIRT	STRETCH POPLIN	220
AMAZING SHIRTS	151234	15TH DEC	NAVY	FRANK LS SLV BUTTON DOWN SHIRT	STRETCH POPLIN	200
FANCY SHIRTS	160223	15TH DEC	GREEN	GRAHAM LS SLV BUTTON DOWN	NEW CHECK POPLIN	150
FANCY SHIRTS	161765	15TH JAN	BLUE	IAN SSLV SHIRT	NEW CHECK POPLIN	200
FANCY SHIRTS	162112	15TH JAN	WHITE	JOHN PLEAT FRONT SHIRT	STRETCH POPLIN	200
AMAZING SHIRTS	162543	15TH JAN	RED	KEITH LS SHIRT	POPLIN STRIPE	100

To production	PP/SS	Received	Fabric	Cutting	Print / emb	Sewing	Washing	Barcode	Finishing / packing	Revise delivery
await andrew pp	no		due 10th Sept	end sept	NONE	1st wk oct	no			
await andrew pp	no				NONE		no			
	PP				NONE		no			
await bob pp	no				NONE		no			
	PP				NONE		no			
	PP				NONE		no			
await eddi pp	no				NONE		no			
	PP				NONE		no			
await bob pp	no				NONE		no			
await bob pp	no				NONE		no			
	PP				NONE		no			
await charlie pp	no				NONE		no			
	SS				NONE		no			
	PP				NONE		no			

WHEN IS IT USED?

Once created, the production team sends the line list to the factories for them to fill in their sections. This sheet is then returned to the production team for their weekly reference. The planning is used all the way through the factories' production procedures, and is sent every week to the production team so that they can see if the pre-production samples have been sent and approved, when the fabric or yarn has been delivered, when it is being cut or knitted, when the labels have arrived and when it has been packed. If any one of the stages has a delay, this can affect the delivery date. For this reason, the production team will be in constant contact with the factories to learn of changes to shipment dates and the reasons for them. The status of these dates is always relayed to the merchandise team who can update the sales teams about possible late deliveries to customers.

KEY SECTIONS

The key sections are:

> **Vendor** (from the line list)
> **Purchase order number** (from the line list)
> **Ex shipment date** (from the line list)
> **Colour** (from the line list)
> **Style** (from the line list)
> **Fabric** (from the line list)
> **Order quantity** (from the line list)
> **Pre-production/size set samples**
> **Fabric/yarn delivered**
> **Knitting**
> **Cutting**
> **Sewing**
> **Washing**
> **Barcode**
> **Finishing**
> **Revised delivery**

In development and production you need to manage the flow of information. If you don't consider yourself organized or able to multitask, choose a different area of the business.

Writing up technical information needs to be clear and precise. Never make assumptions that the factory understands; check and double check everything until they are clear.

As the development matrix is the hub for the style information, keep it updated and without error, as it will reduce problems at a later stage. This is your responsibility.

If you are using more than one factory, be careful when sending the matrix to them. Filter the sheet so that only the information relevant to that factory goes out.

If more than one person uses the planning sheets and you are concerned about other people changing details without your knowledge, password protect it so only you can change details.

10mm

30mm

16385

5/99
3518246
abc-abc

D11015008
SIZE:20X40MM
M873-P188

VI

Chapter 6: **Branding**

Every brand or clothing line has branding and trims on its garments to establish an identity that the customer can come back to. Branding can mean anything from a label sewn at the inside of a garment, embroidery on a shirt or a print across the chest. A trim is a term for the buttons, zips, patches, threads or added items to the garment, which can hold the company's name. For instance, the leather patch with Wrangler or Levi's on the back of a pair of jeans could be classed as a trim. Branding is a multi billion-dollar industry and is in itself a large subject. I am by no means a branding expert, so for the sake of this book, I will keep the subject simple and relevant to the development and production of a fashion collection.

Branding needs to be considered for the first time when the designer is sketching the garments. Trim developments also need to be factored into the timeline and the sketches, so it is important to get a clear direction on new trim developments at this early stage. This can also involve meeting with the trim suppliers to see their new developments. Meetings such as these can often fuel the imagination of the designer, speeding up the process significantly.

The next stage where branding is considered is at the proto review when the designer and the developer approve trim developments and add them onto the proto samples. This, I would say, is a key stage for the branding, as it is the first time you see new garments and trims together. Each is important independently, but together you start to see the brand's collection evolve for the season and this is exciting. It is also possible to amend, add and cancel trims at this stage, whilst still keeping within the time lines for development. I will talk about reviewing the branding in chapter 8.

TYPES OF BRANDING

Branding can fall into two categories: generic or season-specific. Items of branding, like the Ralph Lauren polo player or the Hilfiger flag, remain the same each season, but their colours can change with each new collection. These can be classed as generic, as they are key, recognizable examples of the branding the customer always wants.

DEVELOPING THE BRANDING

Branding ideas that come by way of the concept are season-specific and will change with every collection. Buttons, labels, badges, hangtags and zip-pulls are developed at the start of the season, and are heavily influenced by colour, texture and mood. A highly textured fabric or a distinctive colour within the concept can easily be translated into a trim or branding; alternatively, a bright shade of blue, which may be too intense for a garment, can be perfect for a small woven label or a button. A mock snakeskin fabric may be too expensive to be used in a garment, but can be used as a zip pull for a jacket. To emphasise the aspect of the mood within a concept, the designer may form a concept around a series of old postcards, which can easily be used as prints on hangtags or interior prints on linings. An additional method of adding seasonal specific branding is by adding prints or embroideries to shirts, T-shirts or jackets.

At the same time as the sketches are being made and the development matrix is being created, the design team should also be considering the branding and trim direction of the line.

In general, when it comes to trim and branding development, the developer and designer should discuss new items and ideas with the trim companies while working on the general design concept so as to ensure that the trims will be ready for the finished selling samples. Many of the large fabric fairs (e.g. Première Vision) also have trim halls where you can look at new zip developments and the latest product of the various button manufacturers. Most trim companies will have existing trims that can be adjusted easily for colour and shape, which means that most of the development cost is avoided.

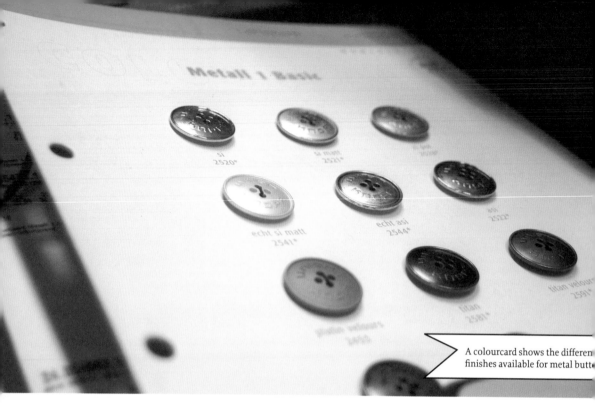

si
2520*

54 mm
2521*

echt si matt
2541*

echt asi
2544*

asi
2522

titan
2581*

titan velours
2591*

A colourcard shows the different
finishes available for metal butto

One area of new development in the trim field is in natural products (leather, wood, corozo or horn) which, although are more expensive and inconsistent in their finish, add a newer element to a garment.

THE DESIGN BRIEF

The designer and developer will meet with the trim company at the start of the development process to discuss ideas on shapes and colours. From this conversation a design brief is formed for the trims or labels. Once the trim company has the final design brief, they will make a prototype for the designer to consider. This could be in the trim company's available fabrics and colours rather than in those specific to the brands. If it is a non-woven trim (button, snap or zip pull) then something called a mould needs to be created.

A mould for a metal is a shell into which the trim material is poured and from which comes a button or metal tag.

For leather patches or woven labels, moulds or plates are still used, but in the sampling stage a temporary mould is used to keep the development costs down. One point to note is that once the mould or screen is set up during development, it is unlikely that another one will be needed for production unless the size changes in the review process. This means that usually the cost of the mould or screen is a one off charge and can be offset against a production order. If there is no production order, you will be invoiced for the development costs.

APPROVAL SAMPLE

Once the artwork is approved then a sample is made and sent to the designer. At all stages the designer has to approve the item before a small sample or production quantity (also known as a run) of the item can be made.

At this stage an article code, like a proto number, will be given to the trim item, and this will be used in the tech pack (if the trim proto number is ready in time) or at the proto review.

TRIM GUIDE
It is common at this point for the development team to make a trim guide for the factories. This can be a simple Excel sheet comprising a picture of the trim, the code and the price per item. The guide is updated by the developer as necessary, and can also

be used to keep track of all sample quantities ordered from the trim company.

CALLING OFF TRIMS
Calling off trims is a term used when a factory contacts the trim company and requests the trim order to be sent to them. Once the trim company makes a large quantity of a button, it will hold it in its warehouse and wait for the 'call off' requests. Having the right labels and buttons in stock is crucial for the best use of time in the production process. If the factory only makes enough for each order, the lead-times for a trim order will always be four to five weeks. If there is stock, the order can be sent the same day.

EXAMPLE

- -

If a brand has a special label for the interior of the garment, they can order 10,000 of the labels to be made at the trim company, knowing that for the first season they may only use 4000. This leaves 6000 left over, just in case they need to make more garments urgently. The factory will

contact the trim company and 'call off' the 4000 they need and the rest will be held in stock. Usually, if you have to remake stock of a label, it can take up to a month, and this could be too long for the factory to wait. Stock levels at trim companies are checked every few months.

- -

TIMESCALES

Needing less time than fabric, trims can take 3-8 weeks to develop and the same to produce, and is, therefore, another key element, which needs to be factored into the planning. Here are the different types of branding and their respective development times.

> **Initial prototype:**

Metal buttons can take 3-4 weeks to develop because of the need to create the mould.

Woven labels can take 2-3 weeks to develop. No mould is necessary, but screens and yarns need to be set up and woven.

Leather patches can take 3-4 weeks to develop. Printing and embossing plates need to be set up and sometimes the brand requires the patches to be washed.

> **Sampling**

Once the proto is approved, sampling quantities can be manufactured in 3-4 weeks. Of course, this is dependent on the complexity of the label and on the order quantity.

> **Production**

Once approved, production can take 4-5 weeks, again depending on the complexity of the style and on the size of the order.

TRIM TESTING

Just as fabric undergoes testing, so do trims. This can either be carried out by the brand or by the trim company. The testing can take between 2-3 weeks, it is carried out between the 'salesman' and production stages, are costed into the final trim price, and are carried out by a third party testing facility or by the trim company itself.

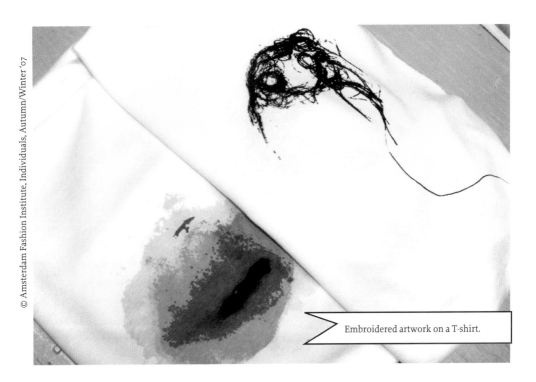

Embroidered artwork on a T-shirt.

TRANSPORTATION

In general, the most cost effective method of transporting the trims between manufacturer and brand is by sea/road, as the air shipment costs add a substantial amount to the cost price of the trim. However, in urgent cases when the trims are needed quickly, shipment by air is the only method.

VARIABLES

With any development and subsequent production there are variables within manufacturing, which the developer needs to accept. In the case of trims and branding, key variables are:

> **Complexity of style**
A simple woven label is easier and quicker to make than one that is embroidered with beads.

> **Base material**
An unusual material needs to be tested and approved for all end-markets before it can be used. Countries like Germany have very strict laws on materials of trims and the dyes used. Check local legislation.

> **Location of manufacture**
To produce in and deliver from the Far East takes longer than from Europe.

> **Size of item**
An unusual size of item will need specific mould and screen sizes compared to a generic size.

PRINTS AND EMBROIDERIES

At the same time that the fabrics and colours are being selected and booked, the design team starts to make the artworks for any prints and embroideries that they want to see in the collection. As mentioned earlier,

these are great examples of season-specific branding, and are sent with the tech packs to the factories with the expectation that strike offs (an example of the print on an available fabric) will be available at the proto review, along with the actual garments. It is not uncommon to develop a lot of different options of both prints and embroideries, so that there is a big selection to choose from at the proto review.

BRANDING THE SAMPLES

Branding the samples means adding trims, labels, prints and embroideries to the styles you are developing. This is done by the designer and the developer at the tech pack creation for the generic labels and also at the proto review stage for the season specific ones. I mentioned earlier in this chapter that most brands have very specific generic branding that they always use; this includes interior and size labels, branded jeans buttons and hangtags. In many cases, brands are really precise about where their labels should be attached on the garment; many have a branding information pack that they send

to their factories about the exact placement of the labels. Take the example of the small red flag label on a pair of Levi's jeans. The position of this label is exact, not randomly placed. If the labels are not applied correctly, the garments are classed as 2nd quality products (see chapter 7).

LABELS

At this point let us take a deeper look at the overall label requirements of the garments, and not just at the external branding.

LABEL INFORMATION

For apparel, the following information is needed somewhere on the interior of a garment:

> **Country of origin**
> **Fibre content**
> RN / CA **numbers**
> **Care instructions**
> **Special hangtags**
> **Manufacturer's details**

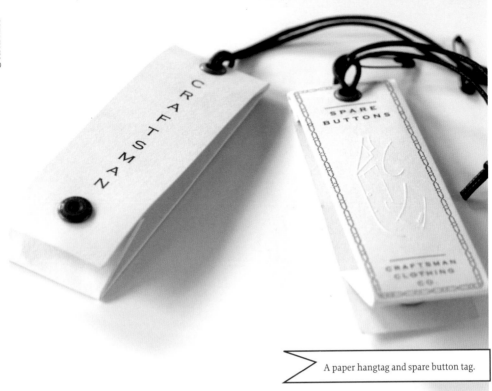

A paper hangtag and spare button tag.

COUNTRY OF ORIGIN
This should be permanent and is usually found on the wash care label or on the size label. If you are selling goods to the USA or to Canada, their strict importing regulations require you to add the country of origin on the size label; however, for the EU, it is sufficient to have it placed on the wash care label.

FIBRE CONTENT
This can be non-permanent, but is usually found on the wash care label.

RN/CA NUMBERS
This is for import purposes for the USA (for the RN) and Canada (for the CA) and is found on the wash care label. The RN and CA codes are used to identify that the company is registered to manufacture a textile or wool product. The company code is unique. If you don't have an RN or CA number then the company name can be printed on the wash care instead.

CARE INSTRUCTIONS
This should be permanent and is on the wash care label. Additional care instructions, which are fabric/garment specific, can either be found on an additional label next to the wash care, or on a hangtag. Examples of these are if fake fur is used, if an embellishment to the garment, such as beading, is more than 15% of the garment, or if the filling of the garment is down/feather.

SPECIAL HANGTAGS
These are used to highlight a feature of the garment; for instance, if there is a special creasing feature on a shirt, many companies

would add a 'special finish' hangtag, which highlights to the customer that the creasing is intentional and not a poor finish from the factory.

MANUFACTURER DETAILS

These are found next to the wash care label. This is called a 'time label' by some companies, and is used to identify the month of production and also the production facility. More details on this later.

INTERNAL GARMENT LABELS

WASH CARE LABELS

Wash care labels are information-rich items, and can be as complicated or as simple as necessary. Brands that sell internationally have many layers of wash care labels, while some have a simple one-sided label. Again, I will stress that this is subject to the policies and practices of each company, but in

general, it will have some of the following information:

> **Company name**
> **Fibre content**
> **Care symbols for the** US **and** EU (if shipped to both regions)
> **Care instructions in writing**
> **Care instructions in symbols**
> **Contact number** (in case of a customer claim)
> **Company address**
> RN **and** CA **codes** (used for export/import purposes)

Usually, the factory will order the wash care labels from a specialist label company, although it is possible to print them within the factory as well. If a brand wants to have the same quality label for all its production, they will nominate a company specializing in wash care labels and each factory will order from them directly. The fabric that the label is printed can vary in cost and in quality, and it is usually the brand that sets the requirements at this level. Ideally, it is a soft polyester satin that is used, since this label will be placed inside the garment next to the skin; however, there are many companies that go for cost over quality, and in some clothes you can find tough, paper-type material with the details printed on; in this case the customer would most probably cut the label out once the garment was at home.

Before production starts, usually during the pre-production sample stage, the factory will suggest specific wash care instructions for the style (which are dependent on the fabric and the garment itself). It's the brand's responsibility to approve their suggestions or offer alternative codes or symbols.

TRUE STORY

A cotton T-shirt doesn't really have to have a hand wash symbol on its care instructions, as it can usually be washed at 30 or 40°C; however, if the T-shirt has a beaded appliqué or complicated print on it, the factory may suggest a hand wash symbol to cover themselves if the print or beads come off. The customers may decide themselves that as it is a cotton T-shirt they can wash it at 40°C, but will undoubtedly be angry if the beads fall off. In this case the company is covered against any legal action, as they clearly suggested a gentle wash treatment.

Another good example is for a suit jacket. The jacket may be cotton and may be unlined, but the factory would probably suggest a 'dry clean only' symbol to be used. Why is this? The jacket is cotton, so it could be washed at home. It is strongly suggested that a suit jacket be professionally cleaned, because it has a complicated construction on the shoulders or around the collar, which could be damaged or become misshapen in washing. For this reason a 'dry clean' symbol would be suggested.

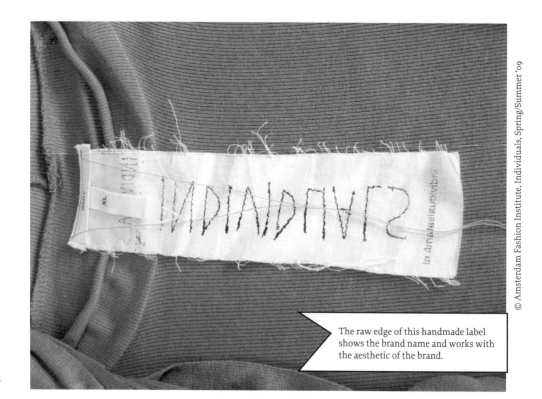

The raw edge of this handmade label shows the brand name and works with the aesthetic of the brand.

TIME LABEL

Sometimes underneath the wash care label there is another small label, which has a series of numbers on it. This is called a time label, and is there to identify the factory, the purchase order of the garment, the month and year the garment was made, and also the style number. This is a locally made label, and the factory can take full ownership of its construction. Why is it necessary? If there is a problem with the garment, perhaps all the buttons fall off on all the jackets delivered, the store can contact the brand to make a complaint and will have the time label information to give to the brand so they can identify the factory that had the button problem.

Sometimes there is more than one factory that makes a product for the brand. Let us say that the brand is making pairs of trousers and it is the best selling line, and the order is for 20,000 pieces. For one factory this quantity could be too high, and as they have no spare capacity, the lead-time for the production would be too long; so, the brand splits the order between two factories to share the risk. If some of the trousers shrink or the zips break, then the brand can immediately identify which factory it came from, and make a claim against the faulty goods. In such a case the time label is invaluable.

The exterior branding and packaging for a product shows the barcode in various guises.

THE BARCODE INFORMATION

In most cases, large brands work with a barcode to display their price and size information. Once the purchase order is issued by the brand, the information on the order relating to style, colour, size and quantity is sent electronically to the barcode company who then prints the barcode stickers and sends them directly to the factory making the garments. Sometimes the barcode is printed on a label and hung next to the hangtag and sometimes it is printed on a sticker and placed on the hangtag. The factory will then follow the brand's instructions as to the placement of the barcode. Whatever the location, the fact is that the price and size information needs to be clear and visible to the member of the general public who will buy the item.

COMPANY LABEL

The company label can be a printed or woven label, and is usually found at the interior of the garment, and usually, in an obvious place for the customer to see it and recognise the brand. For a jacket, shirt or T-shirt it can be found inside at the back of the neck, whereas on trousers or skirts it may be on the inside of the waistband.

SIZE LABEL

This is another label, which generally matches the quality of the company label and is mostly placed near to the company label. This label holds size information of the product, and is sometimes in numbers and letters (alpha/numeric = xs/0, s/2, m/4). The size coding can vary between brands; for instance, French brand Agnes B, uses the sizes 1, 2, 3, etc. for its women's range; some

American companies use 0, 2, 4, 6, 8, for the sizes and Italians use 34,36,38,40, etc.

It is important to note that with this label some countries require it to have the country of origin for import purposes. Countries, such as the USA or Canada, require the combined size and country of origin label to be easily visible on the garment when it is packed. Without this combined label it is impossible to import garments to these countries, and as a result they will get stuck at customs until new labeling is submitted.

EXCEPTIONS FOR LABELS

Of course it is very important to point out that not all product groups need every label to be attached. Some items, like bags and belts, don't have care instructions and to state a fibre content is also optional, whereas wearing apparel is stricter and has more requirements. However, this is specific to the particular brand and the countries they sell in. In this case it is best to check local legislation.

MANAGING BRANDING FOR PRODUCTION

Once the merchandisers have received all the order quantities from the sales teams, and the purchase order has been sent from the brand to the factory, the production planner within the factory will start to order all the trims and labels needed. Sometimes brands take ownership of the trim ordering themselves, so that they have more control over the exact quantities ordered, but in other cases, the responsibility is left with the factory. If you have a choice in this, it is better to let the factory order what they need, as it saves you time not having to calculate all the trim quantities for every order.

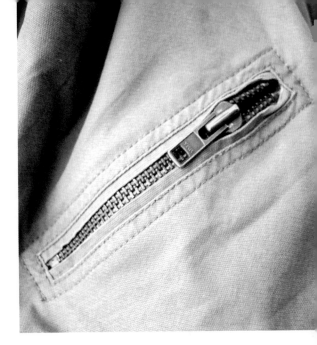

WHEN TO ORDER THEM

It is important for the labels and trims to be ordered as soon as the purchase order has been received, so that that everything is received by the factory and is in hand once production starts, enabling all the different elements of the garment to be placed in the correct order at the sewing stages.

The trims of the garment are attached as the garment is made. The wash care and time label are attached in the side seam, so if the factory hasn't yet received it, the garment cannot be stitched. The zip for a pair of jeans needs to be attached as the front and back legs of the jean are sewn together; it can't be attached at the end. A satin piping is inserted into the waistband of a pair of trousers when the waistband is attached, not once the garment is finished. All it takes is for the wash care label to be late or incorrect, and all production of that piece will stop. If any of the above items are not ready at the start of production, nothing can proceed and there will be a delay.

APX87

CK COPPER / GLOSS LACQ

- -

Branding is big business and possibilities are endless. There are no rules as to what works and what doesn't, so think and work accordingly. Collaborate with the designer with trim ideas.

Understand the identity of your company's brand. Some companies use a lot of branding, whilst some use very little. Recognizing the 'handwriting' of the brand will make it easier when adding branding to the garments.

109

Appreciate the timescales and costs involved in developing and producing trims, and add this into the schedule and cost price.

Always monitor stock levels for the trims. Don't be the one who forgets to reorder labels, as this could halt production.

Learn the local import regulations for internal labeling. Having a production order stuck in customs because of missing information is not acceptable.

- -

VII

Chapter 7: **Factories**

Without factories the world would have no 'stuff'.
It really is a simple as that; we would have no clothes,
no toys, no cars and no books. Referring to themselves
as factories, manufacturers, vendors or sources, they
are all technically the same entity: they all produce items
that are sold in stores. Every factory brings something
different to the process, it could be a better price or a
better quality or more exciting print techniques, so it is
important to be looking for factories all the time.

If you are starting a brand from scratch, the first time the factory gets involved in the process is when they agree to work with you. After that, the next stage is usually the handing over of the initial technical pack to make the prototype. However, the more the factory understands about who you are as a brand and what the concept direction of the new collection is, the more they can help you to realize the designer's vision. I would always recommend sharing some aspects of the concept with them, so that from the outset they can be aware of the types of shapes and styles they will be called upon to make.

MANUFACTURER TYPES

I will be looking at two different types of manufacturers you can work with when developing a range: the factory and the atelier studio.

FACTORY
A factory is a manufacturer that has sample and production lines to meet the needs of both the developments and the bulk production. Within the production lines each machinist works on one stage of the garment only, rather than making the whole garment. The factory is usually set up with fabric, trim and quality departments,

and works on a large commercial scale with brands. In most cases they will have production minimums that the brand needs to meet (much like the case with fabric). Examples of brands that use factories include Tommy Hilfiger, G-Star and Pepe Jeans.

ATELIER

An atelier is a small to medium sized workshop set up for high end, luxury products. An atelier works with an artisan approach, meaning, that in most cases the fabric is cut by hand instead of on automated cutting tables. They are not set up for huge production quantities, and since the cost implications for the service are huge, using an atelier is only suited to a catwalk line or a small label. Compared to a traditional factory that has production lines, an atelier studio has sample machinists that make full garments rather than just a single section of the garment. If any of the technical stages of the garment construction are not correct, they would simply recut the garment and start again. Examples of brands that use an atelier studio are Gucci and Hermes.

TRUE STORY

I have worked for many years with various types of factories, ranging from large Far East ventures to small, family run European companies, all of whom needed a technical pack with a sketch, measurements and detailed instruction on accessories and branding to assist the development process both up to the proto stage and beyond. Usually, at a proto review around 20% of the styles are approved at the first sample, whilst many have to be remade or have measurements changed, prompting adjustments and 2nd proto samples. In contrast, with the atelier studio, we handed over illustrations with few or no measurement instructions. At the proto review 4 weeks later, around 5% had to be remade; the balance were approved. There is a huge difference in the way they work and also in their level of experience.

Some factories have the capabilities of making everything from the fabric to the end product.

FINDING NEW FACTORIES

Finding or sourcing new factories is essential to expand your vendor base. If you are already working at an established brand, they will have a network of factories already working with them, but if you wanted to expand that network, or if you are starting your own company, you have to find new sources. How does one go about this?

ASK OTHER FACTORIES
The easiest way is to ask fabric companies or fabric agents for a factory recommendation. They have very strong links to factories and will be happy to pass your details on to a factory. It will usually mean they will get more business from either you or the factory.

You could also ask factories you already work with for tips, providing you are not looking to take all your business to the competition. Most factories are based in the same area of a city or a country, and because the manufacturing industry is small and interconnected, there is nothing wrong with asking a suiting factory if they know of a good shirt factory. Local agents or buying offices specializing in factories rather than fabric mills also have huge networks of factories and can help select the right one for you.

RESEARCH TRADE FAIRS
Collect as much information as possible at manufacturing and fabric trade fairs. These are great venues to select sources. Whatever the case, don't be afraid to ask.

TYPES OF RELATIONSHIPS

The nature of the relationship you have with a factory can vary. You can have direct relationships with factories or atelier studios, or you can choose a relationship with a factory via an agent or a buying office. Relationships with ateliers are often direct.

DIRECT RELATIONSHIPS

Direct relationships with factories are simple. The fact that it is called a 'direct' relationship means that you communicate directly to the factory manager or their account manager. There is a clear and transparent line of communication. One of the more complicated aspects, and technically a drawback, of a direct relationship is that a common language may be rare or non-existent. In some cases the vendor may operate in a country where English is not a primary language, and without a common language the verbal and written communication becomes difficult, causing potential difficulties for the end product. This could become significant in that if you have serious problems with the factory you have to communicate this directly to them, whereas in an indirect relationship there is an agent or buying office in place to take on this unpleasant task.

INDIRECT RELATIONSHIPS

AGENT
A relationship conducted through an agent has both definite advantages and disadvantages. An agent is usually a one person operation whose aim is to introduce the factory to the brand and provide a basic level of interaction between the two parties. An agent local to the area of the factory can be your connection point to it and can make the business connections on your behalf swifter and clearer, especially where English is not a first language. Your agent will do a lot of the hard work for you in finding the factories, negotiating terms, costs and minimums, and can also provide a translation service for you when it comes to the more technical matters.

The downside to using an agent is that, as they are a small operation, the quality control, trim and label management and financial matters need to be handled by the brand itself.

BUYING OFFICE
A buying office operates in a similar manner as an agent, but is a larger organization comprising account managers who can take sole responsibility for the brand's account, trim departments who can order local trim supplies, quality control who can visit the factories continually throughout production to check orders, and also a finance department who can (under instruction from the brand) make payments to local suppliers for goods (which are later invoiced back to the brand). It is usually located at a major manufacturing centre that will facilitate ordering, communications and oversight for you.

The downside to working with buying offices is that you pay for the service they provide and that you miss out on the direct communication with the factory itself. It is simply an extra link in the chain that is not always needed.

Agents and buying offices will, of course, charge you for their extensive services; they can charge anything from 5 to 10% on top of the cost price of the garment. There are many ways that the finances can be arranged. One method is that they charge you a one-off

115

	Pros	Cons
Direct relationship	Clear communication Builds long term relationships no middle man involved No extra cost added on to FOB	Potential language barrier Having to communicate directly even if things aren't going well
Atelier	Direct relationship No middle man involved Clear communication	Potential language barrier Expensive luxury option Time consuming as not mass market
Agent	No language barrier Local knowledge Access to greater resources Smaller team working for you	Added % to the final cost Greater chance of error with another voice involved
Buying Office	No language barrier Local knowledge Access to greater resources Logistic set up and financial assistance Larger team working for you	Added % to the final cost Greater chance of error with another voice involved

development fee, and have additional charges linked to the size of the production orders arising from this development (10% of the value of production). Their charges can be invoiced directly to you at the end of a season or it can be added into the cost price a factory offers you.

If it is possible, work directly with a factory. If it's not possible, build a strong relationship with an agent / buying office. They are your eyes.

HOW TO JUDGE FACTORIES

What makes a factory good is difficult to describe and identify. In my opinion, a successful factory has a varied client base, offers strong support to the client, has strong local links and they are honest and direct in their relationship with you.

THEY HAVE A VARIED CLIENT BASE
Having a varied client base and covering every market from mass to luxury level gives factories an understanding of every customer and this will reflect in their workmanship. If they can manage a catwalk line in addition to corporate uniforms, they can manage anything that comes in between.

THEY OFFER STRONG SUPPORT
Good factories have a strong back office team consisting of account managers, merchandisers and quality control people. They are the contact people for the brand, and they make sure that all instruction from the brand right through to the machinist is clear, logical and technically correct. They pre-empt possible timing issues and look actively for solutions.

THEY HAVE STRONG LOCAL LINKS
Good factories have strong local links with fabric mills, trim companies and print houses. They are looking at all times to expand their business and look for new opportunities, but not to the detriment of their existing brand customers.

THEY ARE HONEST AND DIRECT
Whether you work with a large established factory or small start-up fabric mill, factories and mills are there to take instruction from the customer. They need clear, concise and reasonable instructions to manage their job, and you should expect them to be honest and direct about their capabilities in return, meaning that they can deliver the expected quality and quantity at the agreed time and price.

WHAT MAKES A BAD FACTORY
Factories make their money from production orders. They spend thousands of dollars / Euros on developments for brands, knowing that they will recoup their investment in making the samples with a production order. Therefore, if the development sample looks great, but production is late, badly made and only half shipped, it is wise to run a mile and never to have anything to do with them again.

Can you, the brand, afford to work with an unreliable factory? Do you, the brand, have the time to hold the factory's hand through every stage so that you get the finished goods you are paying for? Can you afford to have badly made garments shipped one month late? The answer to all the above questions should be no.

Do your research carefully, get recommendations from wherever you can, and do test developments in factories to make sure their products, communication and price match your expectations.

THE END OF A RELATIONSHIP

The basis to any successful relationship is founded on trust, honesty and respect, including in the garment industry. Factories and the relationship between you and them is a very personal one, and whereas it can take years to build up a good understanding, it can take minutes to break it. Ending relationships with a factory is never nice, but it is part of the job.

Sometimes it is a mutual decision; their prices may be too high and your quantities too low. At other times it maybe due to poor performance in one stage of the process which after repeated seasons has not improved, and sometimes it is a management decision at a higher company level that has nothing to do with the performance of the manufacturer, but is something you just have to do. It is never pleasant, but the news is better coming from you in person or on the phone rather than by an email. Business is business, it is not personal.

TRUE STORY

I worked for a brand that closed down its business after three years. The management's decision was final and I, along with my colleague, had to call all fifteen of our factories and tell them the bad news. Some of the factories were large and had many customers, but others were small, family units who relied primarily on our business. It was a hard thing to give them the news, but even

harder to receive it. Because the industry is small, I found myself working again with many of the factories some years after making those difficult phone calls. In the initial phone call years after the brand closed there was no mention of the previous history in the conversation, just the new project I was proposing and the willingness of the factory to start researching fabrics and ideas.

LOCATION

In past years there was a definite location advantage to certain fabric types. China used to be the 'go-to' location for price and quality for most fabrications (cotton and wool specifically), but with the recent shortage of cotton and wool, and the consequent increase of raw material costs, this has meant that China is struggling to hold this title. Sourcing nearer to home, with lower lead-times, is now more in favour. The raw material cost is still the same within Europe, but with the shorter

shipping times and lower Incoterms (see chapter 8) it becomes a more viable option for manufacturing.

With the world seemingly getting smaller, you'll find that this is no longer a real deciding factor. In general, I recommend that you have a combination of sources, some close and some far away. For the purpose of this book I am using the examples of Europe and the Far East as sourcing locations, but you can also manufacture in India, Thailand, North Africa, Brazil, USA, UK, Australia and New Zealand.

The making of a proto sample in a factory sample room: pinning the sleeve of a shirt.

Factories in Indonesia and India are in some cases lower in cost, but they usually expect large order quantities (high minimum quantities) and the shipping time is anything from 4 to 6 weeks. If you are based in Europe and are looking at more local sources, the prices from Italy and Portugal can be comparatively higher than the Far East counterparts, but the order quantities can be lower (with lower minimum quantities) and the shipping or transportation is faster and cheaper.

FACTORY STYLE ALLOCATION

Deciding which factories are going to make your collection starts with building the sourcing plan. The plan lists what factories are used and how many styles they will be asked/invited to develop and produce.

THE SOURCING PLAN

Making a sourcing plan is like putting together a jigsaw. If I were to make one, I would approach it by taking a piece of paper and across the top write the product groups (shirts / jackets / skirts). Under the product groups, using the shirts as an example, I would write the shirt factories we work with: factory A, factory B and factory C. Factory A is an old and established factory; I would give them a high quantity of shirts to make, because I know how they work and because I find them reliable. Factory B is new, so I would give them slightly less than A and for factory C, I would give the fewest as they are a new relationship.

When building a sourcing plan, you should be allocating the styles evenly between the factories, so take the time to distribute their allocation into the basic, mid and top styles, making sure they all have more basic styles than top styles. The reason for this is that whilst the top styles are exciting to work on, the basic styles get the bigger orders and all factories want to have a good mix of exciting and volume. I find that pen and paper work very well, but you can also make a sourcing plan on an Excel chart; there may also be fancy programs that help on this, but I don't know of any. It is all down to experience and knowledge of the factories and the styles that you are working with. Be aware of the location issue here as well.

TRIALING STYLES

Every season it is a good idea to carry out some trials in each product group to continually extend your supplier base. There are no guarantees with factories and anything can happen (fires, floods or bankruptcy), which means it is always best to have in reserve factories that can develop and produce your garments. To trial a few styles with a factory in development and also production takes time, a minimum of one year or so, so patience and trust are needed from both sides.

ALLOCATING STYLES

After making the sourcing plan, you get to the stage of the factory style allocation, which consists of deciding the exact quantity of styles and the level (basic, mid or top) for each factory; for example: factory A gets 5 shirt styles, factory B gets 6, etc. The allocation should always follow the range plan for quantity, and as a result can change throughout a collection's lifespan.

Let us take a look at the factory style allocation of some men's shirts. We have sixteen shirt styles in total, with six being basic, six in the mid section and four being top end styles. For this range of shirts I have invented three different factories, all with their strengths and weaknesses.

> **Amazing Shirts Company**

The Amazing Shirt Company is based in Europe. They are a well-established factory and can handle every price point of shirts from basic to top. They are a fully vertical set up, which means they can handle everything from producing and dyeing fabric to shipping the goods. This is our chief vendor, and one which should have a larger share of the shirts than the other two. They should have a good mix of basic, mid and top styles, thus giving them volume in production (from the basic) to compensate for the top styles (aspirational purchases, which push the brand direction, but give rise to smaller orders).

> **Fancy Shirts and Blouses Ltd**

Fancy Shirts and Blouses Ltd is based in the Far East. They have been a supplier for two seasons, and have shown themselves to be competent in development and production. They can handle middle and top end styles and, although they cannot advise on design aspects, they do provide costings as FOB which, as will be mentioned in chapter 8, means that the cost price they give includes everything. This is our second vendor when it comes to style allocation, and will get a good mix of mid and top price styles to develop.

> **Crafted Garments Ltd**

The Crafted Garments Ltd is also based outside Europe. They are a new supplier, so they need some help getting used to our way of working. They are focusing on basic styles at the beginning, and as a result we will give them two styles to work on as a trial to see how they go. They are a small operation without the capacity to help on design or pattern development, so we would need to give them paper patterns for both the styles. As they aren't set up

for ordering fabric, they will cost the shirts on a CMT basis (they don't include the fabric cost). If we progress with this factory, we will ask that they expand their offer to manage the fabric buying as well, as this is better for us, the brand. However, in the short term, we want to see what they can make and how good the communication is.

We are going to 'double proto' some styles with Crafted Garments to see how the perform; this means that two of the styles that we place with the Amazing Shirts Company will also be put into work with Crafted Garments. Sample both of them at the proto stage so that we can then evaluate which shirt is better for quality and price.

If they both perform well, we will choose the newer factory to give them an opportunity to see the development through and finish with production if the style is selected at launch. If the style doesn't do well in comparison, we would, in this case, just proceed with Amazing Shirts Company and Fancy Shirts and Blouses for the range. This is not ideal, and leaves us with just two factories, but we cannot risk having a badly made, expensive shirt in our range, just so that we have three factories. After all, this is not a charity operation, it is a business.

The main thing to note here is that when you are planning a range, each product group should have at least two potential factories where the product can be manufactured. By having more than one factory you spread the workload and the risk, and also have competition between them, leading to better prices and faster deliveries.

THE FACTORIES' ROLE

The role of the factory is to make the samples and to manufacture the products for the brand. We know that they are involved with the brand from the beginning of the development process, but what are the various stages and what should the factory be doing to solve any problems arising during the process?

PROTOTYPING SAMPLES
From receiving the tech pack from the developer, the factory will make a prototype

sample, which will later be reviewed by the developer, the designer and the merchandiser. The proto sample should be a true representation of the designer's sketch, and should include the items requested in the pack. Sometimes the designer may request something on a sketch that is technically impossible, or perhaps a too great a challenge for the factory. The sign of a good factory is when they offer up solutions to difficult garment constructions rather than admit defeat. "The impossible we do immediately, the miraculous takes a little longer."

CREATING THE COST PRICES

Throughout the sampling process the factory will be calculating the cost price of the garment for the developer. This price will take into consideration the fabric, the construction and the trims (as I have already mentioned in chapter 6). If the factory understands the target market of the brand and is familiar with their product, they will make the developer aware of any price implications on fabric choices or difficult constructions, and in some cases will make alternative suggestions to bring the price down, if they feel it is too high for the brand.

TRUE STORY

- -

I worked with a designer who designed a man's shirt that had a complicated origami construction on the front button placket. For the salesman samples it took a technician one day to make each construction, as it had to be made by hand, since it was impossible

to make by machine. The cost for production was very high, and although it was produced, the order was low and the profit margin was terrible. These issues are discussed between the factory and the developer, so that solutions can be found.

- -

Large scale manufacturing:
in the cutting room.

MAKING THE SALESMAN SAMPLES

At the salesman stage the factory will have already made the proto sample, so it is familiar with the style, the changes that have occurred so far, and what is required in the finished sample. At the proto stage they will make just one sample, but for the salesman sample they can make anything between three and fifty samples, depending on the size of the brand. This takes planning from the factory side and also an understanding of whether garment constructions on one sample can be duplicated.

PLANNING PRODUCTION

The production planning is discussed in the chapter on the flow of information, which includes the key steps the production team needs to take to achieve the planned ex-factory delivery date. Below, I list the general stages of production that a garment will go through.

From the minute the fabric arrives on the factory floor there is a long sequence of events before the garment is finished. The factory will know all the stages and how they should be followed. Here they are listed, with comments on the time implications if delays occur.

1 CUTTING

Once the fabric has been received from the fabric mill it is laid out on cutting tables and then cut according to the pattern pieces. The pattern pieces can either be cut by hand or by an automated cutting machine.

2 FUSING

A fusing machine adds bonding or fusing to the back of each fabric piece if it is required for the garment. The fusing can be of different weights, depending on the end use for the pattern piece (heavyweight for a collar or lightweight for a cuff).

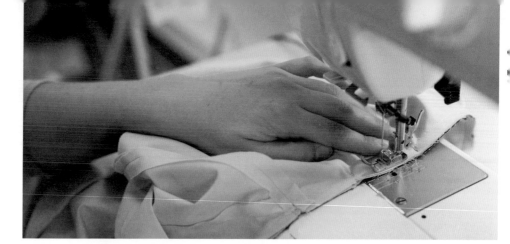

3 EMBROIDERIES AND PRINTS

Embroideries and prints are added to the fabric sections once the fabric has been cut and fused. Embroidery and printing within the production schedule is an important and sometimes time-consuming process, which can have great implications for the end timing. Some factories have their own embroidery and print sections, while others use an external source. Naturally, to use an external source will introduce an additional time requirement that has to be planned for, as they have their own production planning and would, therefore, fit the factory's request into theirs. With in-house printing and embroideries the planning is set at the start of the season and there is no real reason why a delay should occur, thus making it by far the preferred route.

4 SEWING

The main element of production is the sewing line that the garments need to enter. With sewing there are different methods the factories can take, depending on the garment, and also on the nature of their production. With the atelier studio it is not uncommon for one person to make the whole garment from start to finish. This is unusual, and has higher cost and lower productivity than the more general industrial practice of sewing lines, where each person makes a section of the garment and then passes it to the next person for the next stage. This makes for what is known as a production line, and means that one person spends all their time on just one procedure. This method is much faster, and is perfect for a large order of hundreds or thousands of pieces.

5 WASHING

Sometimes T-shirts, sweatshirts, woven shirts and other items in light woven fabrics are washed once sewn, which gives a more 'relaxed look' to the garment. This is not to say that the garment will look crinkled and used, as it will be ironed subsequently; it just softens the fabric after manufacture, and gives a softer hand-feel to the end product. This process can add a minimum of 3 days to the production timings. It is unusual for heavy suiting or coats to be washed with water, as this could affect the fabric and cause shrinkage; however, they are sometimes tumbled to soften the garment for a more relaxed feel.

6 INTERNAL LABELING

Wash care instructions are an often overlooked addition to the garment. The main purpose of the label is to assist in the care of the garment. After all, you may have paid a lot of money for it and don't want it to shrink, melt or end up misshapen after the first wash. The production department works closely with the factory and the fabric mill to establish exactly what should be written on the label. It is the factory's responsibility to have the correct coding, as should there be any claims from the customer about incorrect advice, the factory is liable.

7 EXTERNAL LABELING

Barcodes are on the stickers that are attached on to the hangtag for the stores to swipe when a purchase is made. The hangtag is attached to the garment at the end of the production line before the final quality control, and before they are packed into the poly bags. The sticker or ticket has the style name and the price unencrypted, and is usually produced at an external company and sent to the factory several weeks before the bulk shipment of garments

is due to leave. Sometimes the tickets are late from the external company, and this can cause a huge delay in the end shipment.

8 IN LINE QUALITY CONTROL

Quality control, or QC, is an important component of production. Most brands issue a compliance manual, which is made in conjunction with the country of origin's legal standards. An effective quality control department will stage checks at every stage of the production, so that errors can be spotted and eliminated.

Whereas pre-production samples are usually sent to the brand office for fitting and approval, the size sets are sometimes seen at source during a QC or quality control trip (for instance in the case of denim styles where they have many washes and many sizes).

These trips are carefully planned at particular stages of the process, so as not to delay the final bulk date, but to allow enough time to measure enough garments to get a representative cross section of the bulk. If truth be told, it is the most unglamorous of all the trips, and involves arriving at the factory with a pen and a tape measure and measuring samples of all sizes to ensure they are all within tolerance of the size specification.

What do we mean by tolerance? For each measurement of the garment the tolerance allowed is the amount above or below the specified measurement to allow for human error in cutting or sewing, or for the nature of the fabric. T-shirts and sweater knits are hard to measure accurately, as they are stretchy by nature and can mean that the measurements can be quite different from what you asked for, not because the factory have executed poorly, but because of the particular fabric. Experience will teach you how to work with these garments. Each brand will have a different tolerance allowance. For example, the length of the man's shirt sleeve could be 69 cm; the tolerance that could be acceptable is 1 cm either side.

With a woven fabric the tolerance allowed due to fabric is less, and any mis-measurement could be down to human error. It is important to measure as many garments as possible to see where the problem is. If the poor measurement is in the same spot all the time (e.g. the sleeve is always 8 cm too long) then it is likely that the pattern is not correct. In this case the factory would recheck the pattern, and if it was incorrect, a new one would be made for all subsequent garments; those already produced would have to be corrected and remade. It is a costly mistake, but it is very important that the garment should be as close to the spec as possible. We want it to sell, after all.

On trips like this it is very common to spend the day or maybe even 3 days checking measurements and the construction of all the garments. If at the end of the trip all issues have been resolved on the styles you have checked, they can proceed into production. If, however, there are continuing problems, then more samples need to be made and approved, and this can have an impact on the bulk shipping date. At this point a decision needs to be made by the production team and the merchandiser as to the severity of the issue, and whether it should jeopardise the end date.

10 FINAL QUALITY CONTROL
Once the goods have been produced and the labels attached, the last of many checks is undertaken by the in-house QC team. At this stage the team is checking the finishing, any loose threads, the pressing and the label attachment. If any of these are substandard or questionable, they are rejected and classed as second quality. At this stage, if the QC has managed production correctly, there shouldn't be any real surprises on fit or quality, and if a label has been attached incorrectly, it can be amended and the garment passed. Of course, there are always problems in production – nothing is seamless (no pun intended), but problems can be kept to a minimum with good communication and a good relationship between factory and brand. Regular visits throughout the production process can help hugely. If quality or fit irregularities are spotted at this late stage, the production team at the brand should be informed, as this could result in a remake (which will cause a delay to delivery), or in the worst case, a cancellation.

© Trey Guinn

A poly bag used for packing garments.

PACKING THE GOODS

Once the final checks have been completed and the QC is finished, the goods can be packed in the polythene bags, then into the box cartons ready for shipping.

BAG REQUIREMENTS
Each brand has different conditions and needs when it comes to packing, but in general they use a bag that is recyclable and has the following requirements:

> **Warning instructions in several languages relevant to the market**
> **Perforations to avoid the possibility of suffocation**
> **Black recycle triangle of a specific size and position.**
> **Green circle point recycle sign of a specific size and position.**

The bags can be made locally as long as they have the above warnings and codes.

PACKING METHODS
The type of garment will also dictate how they are transported, which varies according to the type of product, price level of garment, factory location and transport availability. Suits, leather jackets and coats are sometimes packed with a coat hanger and with tissue in the sleeves to hold the garment's shape, whereas a T-shirt or sweater knit would be folded into a flat pack; every brand has different requirements. The decision as to the packing method and packing materials used should be finalized at the early stages of production, so that it can be ready ahead of the finished goods.

The main methods are classified as 'flat' or 'hanging'; however, you can also have 'flat hanging'.

Here are some examples to show the difference:

> **Flat Pack**
  T-shirts
  Sweater knits
  Underwear
  Jeans
  Formal shirts (with supported collar)
  Belts
  Scarves
  Jewelry

> **Hanging**
  (This involves the garments to be hung vertically in an upright box)
  Leather jackets
  Tailored jackets
  Tailored separates
  Outerwear
  Silk shirts
  Dresses

> **Flat hanging**
  (This involves the goods to be placed on hangers but laid completely flat in a long thin box)
  Leather jackets
  Tailored jackets
  Outerwear

BOX REQUIREMENTS

Most brands have specific box or carton requirements that are necessary for their warehousing system. These requirements refer to the size and composition of the box, as well as to the information that is placed on it stating the carton contents and weight.

SHIPPING THE PRODUCT

The goods should be now ready for shipment, with the export paperwork ready, the packing lists completed and the invoices checked. In general, each delivery should have a packing list that lists every item, colour, size and quantity in the box, as well as an invoice with the same information.

SECOND QUALITY GOODS

It is usual for most companies for the second quality goods to be packed separately from the first choice, so that they can be handled in a different section of the brand's warehouse. Second quality goods are items that have been rejected by QC for small mistakes (a small sewing irregularity or a badly attached label). Most brands accept second choice goods at a lower cost price, and will have them checked at their warehouse to establish the problem. In most cases the goods are only very slightly different from the first choice, but it is enough to separate them away from the first choice, so that they aren't allocated to the stores with the first shipment. These goods can still be sold, but will be sent to an outlet store rather than to the main store.

TRANSPORT

Once the goods have been checked and paperwork is completed, the arrangements are made for transportation. The decision would have been made at the development stage and before production started as to the proposed method, as this would greatly affect the final landed price. Goods from the Far East can either be exported by air or sea, whilst those from Europe also have the option of road, depending on the location of the brand's warehouse.

Without factories you have no garments, so a good portion of your time in development and production should be spent finding new factories and trialing styles with them.

Always be clear and honest with a factory in your working practice. The industry is small, and an unprofessional approach will be remembered.

Whenever you can, always visit a factory to understand their capabilities and specialties first hand rather than rely on an email introduction, as this will strengthen the relationship between both parties.

129

Making a style allocation needs flexibility and patience. It will change many, many times, with added styles and changes to fabrics. Don't get frustrated; see it as a giant jigsaw puzzle with more than one solution.

Spend time understanding how a cost price is built up. Once you know this, it is much easier to negotiate with the factory and the designer to get the best end product.

Chapter 8: **Reviews**

Reviews are opportunities for the garments and prices to be assessed at the key stages of developing and producing the collection. At the 'prototype', 'salesman sample' and 'production' stage, the designer, the developer and the merchandiser review the collection together, each from their particular viewpoint. Reviews are necessary not only to check up on the current progress of the garments, but also to refer back to the concept and range plan, which were formed at the start of development.

After handing over the initial tech packs of the styles to the factory, it can take anywhere from 4 to 7 weeks for a first protos to be ready, depending on the complexity of styles and the type of vendor you use. The factory will prepare the prototypes, and if you have denim, they will make leg panels as well (as mentioned earlier in chapter 4).

As the developer, you approach the proto review from a different perspective from that of the designer or the merchandise team, who are also present at the review. You will look at whether the sleeves are too long or the pocket is too high, the designer will look to see if the design is right for the concept, and the merchandise team will be concerned with the overall range plan and the prices.

In an ideal world, it is best to review all the garments of the range together, so that the reviewers can see how all the styles, colours and prices align, but the fact that the initial handover of the styles to the factories is spread out in time, means that you get to review them at different times.

REVIEW CHECKLIST

Before going into the process of the proto review, make sure you have all the paperwork, recording stuff and practical tools to hand. Here is a handy checklist to work by:

> **Paperwork**
> **Practical tools**
> **Organising**
> **Compare to tech packs**
> **Measuring**
> **Recording tools**

> **Paperwork**
  As the review happens, fabrics are checked, changed and added. Colours are swapped and deleted, and new styles added. As a result it is very useful to have all the files ready, so that you have everything to hand. Have all your technical packs together, along with all fabric selections and colour cards. This will mean that you have direct access to the style information and will make the checking part easier. Have a printed out copy of the development matrix split to the factory, as well as a total overview. You will be referring to this constantly, as styles, colours and fabrics are changed. This is also a good place to make notes of added and cancelled styles.

> **Practical tools**
  At the review, the team will also look at buttons, trims and branding ideas, and may pin notes, recording ideas onto the garments, so have pins with you at all times. If the garments need to be cut and adjusted it is also best to have an iron and ironing board on hand to make the finish neater.

> **Organising**
As obvious as this sounds, placing the samples in some kind of logical order makes a huge difference to the flow of the meeting. They can be placed in order of the development matrix, fabric, colour or product group. It is easier to compare like with like together.

> **Compare to tech packs**
I find that a quick reread of the technical packs takes you back to the start of the process, and every conversation you had with the designer is a clear and vivid memory. Remember that the tech packs were made two months earlier, and the small details that were so important back then are sometimes completely forgotten about now. Read through the tech packs,

taking stock of the details and specific requests, ensuring that they have been carried out on the sample; if for some reason they haven't, find out why and have that reason ready when the designer reviews the style. As a developer, you are there not only to support the designer, but also to drive the reviewing process forward.

> **Measuring**
We already know from chapter 5 that a factory has been sent the size spec according to which the sample should be made. Once the proto is made, the factory should check the sample against the requested spec before they send it through for the review, noting if the garment is exactly as specified or whether

Reviewing the sketches ahead of a proto review.

it is out of tolerance (too big or too small), but in some cases there is no time. There are a number of reasons why a garment could be out of tolerance (out of spec), maybe it is the pattern, maybe shrinkage or maybe workmanship. Measuring the samples yourself easily adds another three days on to the trip, but it means that you have a clearer picture of the fit and can conduct the review of the garments more effectively.

> **Recording tools**
Images of the garments will be invaluable once the review is over to remind you what was changed. Have a digital camera with you to record the changes you make in a review.

PROTO REVIEW

The proto review is the first sample that is reviewed by the developer, the designer and the merchandiser. The sample is made by the factory based on the technical pack, and is the first opportunity to review the garment, fabric, branding and cost price.

WHEN DOES IT HAPPEN?
The proto review usually happens around 4-6 weeks after the technical packs have been handed over by the developer to the factory. The proto sample can take anything from 2 to 4 weeks to make, depending on the complexity of the style and type, the lead-time of the fabric and also the size of factory. A large factory with many machinists and a sample room dedicated to making

proto types can make a sample from start to finish in two weeks, but a smaller company may take four, because they have fewer facilities to cater for this. Similarly, a T-shirt will take less time to make than a leather jacket, as there are fewer processes involved in its construction. So, the timing of the review can be variable.

LOCATION

Proto reviews can either be conducted at your office or at the buying office, agent or factory. As with the tech pack handover discussed in chapter 5, doing the proto

review at the factory is always better for focus, and as you have the garments there and its makers to hand, you are really able to concentrate on the matter, free from any distraction. The disadvantage is that you have to transport all your files and materials with you. The review can take from 3 days to 2 weeks, and at times it can be a demanding and frustrating experience. In a matter of days you, the design and the merchandise teams will review the same range that took 3 months to develop. It is an intense time and one needs mental strength and good preparation in order to come

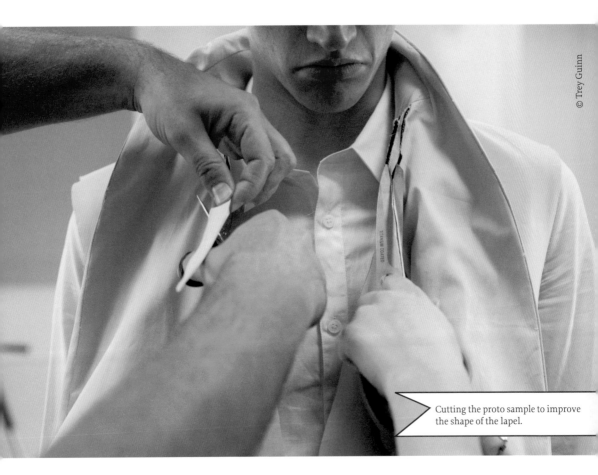

Cutting the proto sample to improve the shape of the lapel.

through it unscathed. You will be exhausted, possibly jet lagged, surrounded by work colleagues and working 14-hour days.

GARMENTS

The review of the garments happens in four stages:

> **Fitting**
  Fitting the samples on a fit model
> **Checking**
  Checking the samples against the technical pack's requirements
> **Changing**
  Changing the styles for the fit or fabric
> **Adding and cancelling**
  Adding new styles or cancelling others that haven't worked in an actual garment

1 FITTING

A proto fitting is an important part of the review, and involves the designer, the development team, the account manager from the factory and a pattern maker either from the brand or from the factory. All the garments need to be fitted on a 'fit model'. Sometimes the brand will take its regular

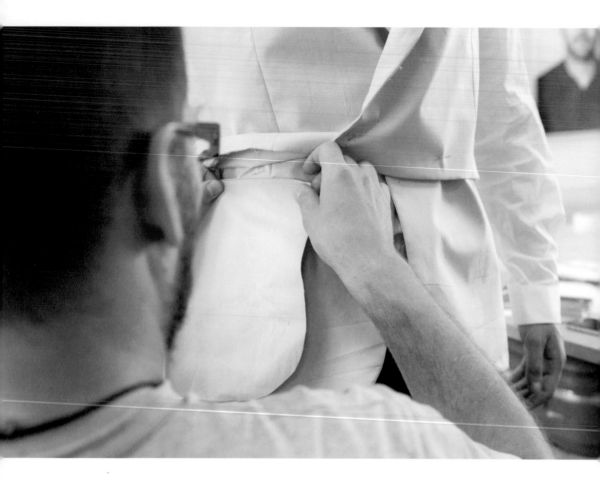

fit model to the proto review and sometimes the model is hired where the factory is based, from a local fit model agency. Whatever the situation, the model should have the same base measurements (or close to it) as you used for the patterns back at the development stage. Remembering that this is a prototype and not a final sample, changes may be made to the fit of the garment, (maybe the neck is too high, maybe the body is too big, maybe the sleeves are too long) and proportions are also adjusted (pockets too high, zip in wrong place, too many buttons). Sometimes the changes and adjustments

are pinned onto the sample and sometimes they are written on with a pen. This is a great method of communicating the exact location of the change and the instruction, and is a permanent reminder for the factories. The pins may fall out of the sample in transit, but the writing will always remain.

2 CHECKING
Check how the garment actually looks on the model. There are many more technical approaches to fitting a garment, but start with the basics, and the rest you will learn with experience.

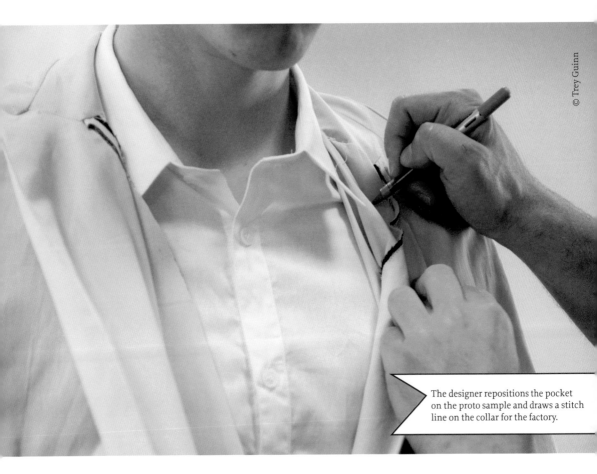

© Trey Guinn

The designer repositions the pocket on the proto sample and draws a stitch line on the collar for the factory.

Let us take two examples: a shirt and a pair of trousers.

› Fitting a shirt
- Does the shirt actually fit?
- Are the sleeves too long?
- Is the collar too tight?
- Is the collar shape even at both sides?
- Does it fit across the shoulders, chest, waist and length?
- Is there a pocket and is it in the correct position on the chest or is it too far under the sleeve and hidden in the armpit?
- Look at the placement of the buttons; do they look evenly placed or do they finish half way down the shirt leaving four inches of open shirt?
- Is the shirt pulling across the shoulder or under the arm?
- Does the shirt fall nicely against the back of the model or does it kick out at the waist and bottom of the shirt?
- When the model lifts his arms, is it too tight or is there room to move?

> **Fitting a pair of trousers**
- Can the model get the trousers on?
- Do they fit on the waist, hip and around the bottom?
- Are the back and front rise comfortable, or does they cut into the body at the front (from button and zip to under the crotch), or the back (around the bottom and under the crotch)?
- Does it fit on the thigh or does it 'hug' the leg too much?
- Do the knee and ankle have enough space?
- Can the model sit down without splitting the trousers?
- If there is a pocket, can the model get their hands inside the pocket?
- Is the pocket bag the correct depth and are the pockets positioned in the correct position?

Once you have established the fit, focus on the fabric and decorative aspects.

> **Fabric**
- Is the weight of the fabric that has been selected by the designer appropriate for the style? Sometimes the fabric can be too heavy for the style and sometimes too light. This affects how the garment 'hangs' on the body.

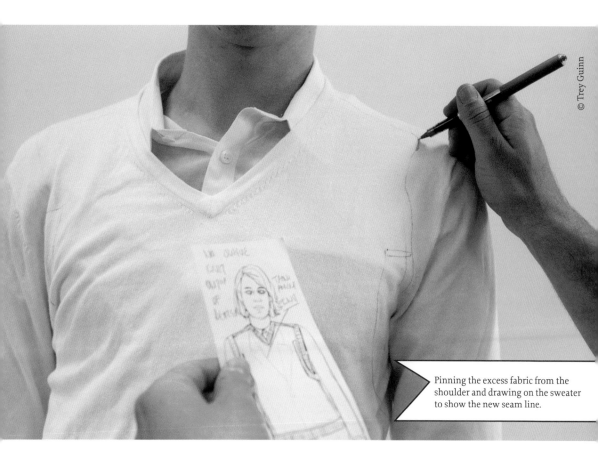

Pinning the excess fabric from the shoulder and drawing on the sweater to show the new seam line.

- Does the fabric colour match the colour card of the designer?

All these need to be assessed and noted. If the fabric is not appropriate, now is the time to change it.

> **Decorative aspects**
  - Is there decorative stitch on the garments? (an embroidery or contrast colour sewing stitch)
  - Is it in a matching colour ('tone on tone') or a contrasting one? What was requested?
  - Does it look nice or is it too contrasting or off tone compared to the request?

- Was branding mentioned on the tech pack?
- Is it there?
- Is the placement OK for proportion and position or is the placement wrong?
- Is there a contrasting coloured fabric used as a trim?
- How does it look?
- Will there be problems of colour bleeding from one fabric into another?

All these points should be discussed between the developer and the designer, so that the placement of the decorative aspects is finalized and clear for the factory.

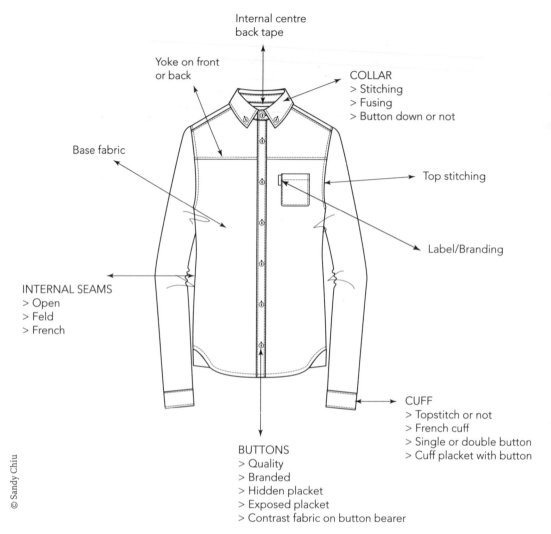

Internal centre
back tape

Yoke on front
or back

COLLAR
> Stitching
> Fusing
> Button down or not

Base fabric

Top stitching

Label/Branding

INTERNAL SEAMS
> Open
> Feld
> French

142

CUFF
> Topstitch or not
> French cuff
> Single or double button
> Cuff placket with button

BUTTONS
> Quality
> Branded
> Hidden placket
> Exposed placket
> Contrast fabric on button bearer

COLOUR BLEEDING

One of the biggest problems of using contrasting fabric as a trim is that one colour can bleed into the other. What do we mean by bleeding? If you put a red sock in a white wash, some of the red dye comes out of the sock into the water, only to be deposited on the white fabrics and you will end up with pink clothes. So, putting

a white fabric on a red jacket or vice versa could have an unfortunate outcome when the customer first washes the jacket at home.

THINK PRACTICALLY

Take the example of the contrasting fabric used as a trim. Be aware of this and if the designer is insistent, use fabrics with stable dyes, or use colours that won't impact on

EXAMPLE

- -

I can never stress enough the importance of making protos in an appropriate colour and fabric. Suppose a shirt that is supposed to be made in a silk chiffon is made in a denim for the proto. You can imagine that the proto will look more like a jacket then a floaty silk shirt. There is a high chance that the proto would get cancelled, as it is too hard to visualise the final effect with the proto in denim.

I was developing a range for a men's casual label and one of the styles was a suit made from a very dense sweatshirt fabric. The jacket was a single breasted jacket and the pants were like a five pocket denim style, but made in a heavy sweatshirt fabric instead. The style was going to be garment dyed in a dark grey colour and then heavily washed so it would have a vintage look. The factory couldn't find a dark coloured fabric to make the proto in, so made it in the only available colour to hand. When we opened the box of protos we found a yellow suit. I laughed, the designer walked out and the style was dropped.

- -

each other; dark colours together or synthetic fabrics work well.

BE FLEXIBLE

Flexibility is the key quality during this stage. Just because something was mentioned on a tech pack doesn't mean it is set in stone. The review is an opportunity to change anything, affecting one style, all the way up to the whole range.

3 CHANGING

At this stage we have fitted the proto (making comments and changes on the technical pack) and we have assessed whether the fabric selected by the designer is a good match to the style. If you think the fabric is too heavy, too light or visually just doesn't work for the garment or the concept, you can look at other fabrics you and the designer have already selected in the range, to see if it is possible to switch to an existing fabric. If it is, then you should make a comment in the development matrix and in the technical pack that the fabric has been changed.

FACTORY ASSISTANCE

Remembering that you don't have the luxury of another eight weeks of fabric lead-time, you need to have stock of the fabric, so that the final samples can be made. In this scenario, the B/O, agent or factory contacts the fabric mill directly to see if there is more of the fabric available for the new samples. If there is availability then the change is workable; however, if there is nothing available in stock then you have to find an alternative. Alternative fabric hangers are requested and assessed for price, lead time and quality. In most cases the proto is made in the final fabric (it may not be the exact colour but the fabric is the final one), which is by far the best situation for reviewing protos, as the drape of the fabric can make a garment look either amazing or terrible. If a substitute fabric is used and is inappropriate for the garment, it will visually kill the style, and there is a high chance that it will be deleted from the range. At this proto reviewing stage it is hard to visualise a finished garment from a proto where the fabric is incorrect

and the fit needs adjustment, as there are too many variables that have to be taken into consideration by the designer and the developer. Bearing in mind that the range is probably overdeveloped anyway, opportunities to cancel a style that doesn't work are welcomed.

4 ADDING AND CANCELLING

Throughout the proto review there is always a possibility of the design team adding styles to the collection either as replacements for existing styles or as true additions. It is likely that the designers will take the opportunity of being in a new city (if you are reviewing at the factory's location) to do some shopping by way of research, and as a result new

ideas may emerge. As with every style, the developer will create a new technical pack as before, and hand over the style to the factory as it is added to the range. They will also add the style to the development matrix.

ONGOING ADJUSTMENTS TO THE DEVELOPMENT MATRIX AND RANGE PLAN

You can imagine from the above that all changes and adjustments have implications for the range plan and the development matrix, and you would be correct. This is why it is so important for the developer to record all the changes as they happen, so that the matrix and range plan can be kept complete and correct at all times.

FINAL OVERVIEW

Once you have all the garments examined at this review laid out, fitted, made of the correct fabric (or its agreed replacement) and branding assigned to each style, you can see how this part of the range looks or should look once all the required changes have been made. Of course, this is probably not the whole range; it is only what comes from this factory or set of factories; if you work with many factories, it is likely that you will encounter exactly the same experiences the following week.

BRANDING

As the developer and the designer are also reviewing the branding of the garments at this stage, it is also an opportunity for them to review the branding options they have developed, and to make suggestions for the location of this branding on the garments.

TRIMS AND BRANDING SAMPLES

At around the same time as the proto review, new trim developments, which were created by the brand when the tech packs was created, will start to be submitted by the trim companies to the developer and the designer. One of each new trim is sent with an approximate price for the designer or the developer to review. The team will compare the trim firstly with the artwork submitted originally to the trim developer to see if it is what was requested, but they will also match it to the prototypes to see if the idea works in reality on the garment. As with the comments on the proto samples, the developer or the designer may supply the trim developer with suggestions for changes or amendments to the trim, so that they can either proceed with a second sample for approval or can proceed to a sample run of the agreed version.

SAMPLE RUN VS PRODUCTION RUN

A sample run is a small quantity of, maybe 50-100 pieces of each trim made specifically for the salesman samples. A production run is a much larger quantity and can run into the thousands. At this stage of the process you should only be asking for a sample run, so that there isn't too much stock left over once the brand's salesman samples have been made.

APPLYING THE BRANDING

The designer and the development teams work together to establish the position of the branding, and then apply it to the proto samples by means of attaching paper photocopies of labels and buttons onto the garments with pins or double-sided tape. For the zips, you can simply note down the required reference code on the garment and on the tech sheet, referencing size, colour and quantity. This application of the final branding location is a clear and accurate method for the factory to follow.

PRINT AND EMBROIDERY STRIKE OFFS

Sometimes the designer will make a design for a T-shirt print or an embroidery that they intend to place on the garment. These prints or embroideries are reviewed in the form of a 'strike off' by the designer and the developer. A strike off is an example of the requested artwork, but in a rough form. It should be in the correct requested size and also in the correct colour, but rather than being on a garment, it is sent on a simple piece of fabric of the same weight and construction as the garment. Sometimes the factory sends several options of the strike off in different sizes or different colours. As with a lab dip mentioned in chapter 4, the developer comments, and either approves it or asks for another version with changes. If the strike off is approved, it will be pinned

TRUE STORY

- -

At a proto review, the CEO of the brand I once worked for decided at 3 p.m. that he hated all the branding we had developed for the men's line and insisted that we changed the colour, size and location of the badges and labels we had sampled. At 9 a.m. the following day I was due to fly to the factory to hand over the styles, so I had to have garments and tech packs

updated for then. Upon hearing the rebranding news, the designer and I took turns at the photocopier, resizing and recolouring all the branding and then placing in the new locations. I finished updating the tech packs around 11 p.m. that night. This was one occasion when I questioned my career choice.

- -

on to the garment in the correct position and also be added to the proto review comments and will be added to the final salesman sample by the factory.

PRICES
Each style that is developed in the range has a factory cost price, which is the factory's cost of making up the garment. The proto review is also the first opportunity for the developer and the merchandiser to see the initial cost prices of the prototypes. There are two different methods of costing a garment; it can either be a CMT price or an FOB price.

CMT means Cut / Make / Trim. This is where the factory only costs these elements in the price, not including the fabric cost. The customer, not the factory, needs to supply this. FOB is a shipping term and means Free On Board, but in the context of the costing it is a term that means the factory pays for the total cost of the goods, the fabric, the cutting, the making and the trims and also some of the transport costs.

Another shipping term sometimes used is CIF (Cost, Insurance and Freight). This is a method of calculating the cost of supplying goods from a manufacturer, which includes

all costs for the garment manufacture in addition to that of transportation to the brand's nominated location (usually the brand's central warehouse).

The majority of brands will work with FOB pricing, as it is the total cost of the garment, and is a more complete price for the developer and the merchandiser to work with. If you work with a CMT price you have to remember to add in the fabric cost, and this can be hard for the developer to calculate. As it is the factory that usually works out the consumption of the fabric (how much is required for each garment) and not the developer, there could be an element of guesswork from the developer's side, which could mean either an insufficient fabric order or over booking.

ACCURATE TARGET PRICES
The retail selling prices are set when the range plan is established, so you already know that for most product groups you will have approximately three tiers of selling prices: the basic, mid and top styles. Sometimes brands send target cost prices through to the factories when the technical pack is handed over, but others prefer not to, as it can restrict the factory in their creative

approach. It is a testament to the skill of the developer and the relationship with the factory, if she can give an accurate price target based on the sketch and the factory comes back with a similar price. In most cases it works out well, but in some cases adjustments need to be made to ensure that there is a logical pricing structure related to the complexity or simplicity of the styles.

MINUTES

The making of every section of the garment is measured or calculated to take a specific number of minutes and each of these have a cost, so the price of the prototype is the first time the minute calculation costing is put together. It is a combination of the fabric cost, the trims involved, the time involved in making the pattern and also the number of minutes needed to make the whole item. For example, the approximate timing used to make a buttonhole by a specialized machine is 0.20 min, but making it by a regular machine can take 2 min. The cost of pressing a zip and side seam in a dress may be 6 mins, but to make a hem for a simple dress could take 0.20min. It is important to note that the prices are for the proto samples before the review. Any changes made in the reviewing process will require the timings/prices to be updated once the factory has received all the developer's comments. This price will go through at least two more adjustments before it becomes final; at this stage the cost price is just an indication.

CHANGES TO IMPROVE THE PRICE

In some cases you may decide to make serious changes in all areas, which could make a significant difference to a price, perhaps taking a style from a basic retail price point to a top retail price. This would have implications on your price build up in the range plan, but if the changes were justified for the sake of the concept, the range plan would be altered to accommodate these changes. If the style has to stay at a basic selling price (for the sake of the range plan)

TRUE STORY

- -

I used to work for a brand that made men's and women's formal clothing. All our manufacturers used to quote me prices in FOB except for one who quoted in CMT. This one factory advised that it wasn't possible to quote in FOB until the final salesman samples had been sewn, all the changes at the review fittings had been made, and the true consumption of the garment had been calculated. This meant that I wouldn't get the final FOB prices from this factory until two months later than from the rest of the manufacturers. In this instance what I had to do was estimate the consumption for all his styles, take the fabric price by meter and calculate the fabric cost, adding an additional amount for buttons, interlining and trims. This gave me an estimate FOB from which my merchandiser could work out our profit margins. Once all the samples from all the factories had been received, and the prices submitted, we then had an accurate set of FOBs from all. But this all came very late and meant that we ended up using an incorrect profit margin for most of the development cycle.

- -

Reviewing samples.

but the changes are too complicated (take too many minutes) then the factory should advise you of possible technical adjustments that can be made to keep the price more commercially viable. Here are two scenarios:

› Scenario 1

In the range there is a basic men's shirt in a cotton poplin fabric with a cuff, no chest pocket and no additional details. At the proto review the designer wants to add a pocket, embroidery, pleats in the back panel and a French cuff (when the cuff turns back on itself). Since all these changes have cost implications, a discussion opens between the developer and the factory.

The first thing to look at in order to find a solution is a breakdown of all these costs from the factory (the costs of the embroidery, the addition of pocket, the cuff change and the pleat addition). This is called an open costing, which consists of the prices of every procedure involved in making the shirt. From these, work out with the merchandiser what the highest cost price is that you can accept whilst still making a profit.

The next step is to look at the fabric that is used; can it be changed for the same quality but at a cheaper price, perhaps to free up some money for an additional pocket? Then think about what a customer would look for in a shirt. Which items that the designer wants to add would 'make or break' a sale? Pleats at the back of the shirt are nice, but few customers go looking for a shirt specifically with a pleated back. However, a pocket and a French cuff could be on someone's wish list (as these make a shirt dressier and look more expensive), so look at these prices and see if you can build them into the cost.

Once you have all the costings and you have a couple of options for compromise, sit down with the designer and the merchandiser and work out a solution that is acceptable to all sides. Most of the time this works, but sometimes the designer will be immovable on the additions and the price will have to go up accordingly.

> **Scenario 2**

A basic shirt style may have a target cost price requirement of between 20€ and 22€ (to hit a good profit margin at retail when sold), but the actual cost price given by the factory may be 28€. How do you approach this problem without completely changing the shirt? Changing the shirt's position in the range plan structure can help, and is often the quickest solution, provided the whole range still comes out as a 'pyramid shape'. If it is essential to keep the same fabric then the shirt should be moved from a basic style to a top price style which holds the target cost of 25 to 30€ (matching the given cost price).

AFTER THE REVIEW

During the proto review the prototype samples will be pinned, cut and written on, so that the designer can realise his vision and the factory can fully understand the changes. Remember that with the majority of the factories English is not their first language, so they need to see a visual marking, photograph or adjustment, as well as a written modification of the tech pack to understand exactly what is required.

DOCUMENTING CHANGES

The designers and the developers take digital pictures of all the styles for reference, so that when they are at other reviews with the remaining garments they have a record of what they already set in work. With so many samples being reviewed at the various sources, it is important to keep a visual reference of all the changes and additions made.

TRUE STORY

— —

I worked on a range that had a double cashmere fleece fabric for a small collection of garments where the fabric price was 197.00€ per meter. When it came to production we had to rework the FOB price to improve the margin, but with such a unique fabric we couldn't completely change the composition or weight so radically as this would alter the finished style, so the same fabric mill offered us a fabric with 80% cashmere rather than the previous 100%, at a new price of 97.00€ per meter. The alternative fabric was half the price but looked the same as the original. We had to compromise on the cashmere percentage, since if it was either this or a cancelled style.

Sometimes it just isn't possible to make the adjustments to the style to achieve the better price. In this case it may be possible to move the style within the range plan to keep the styling of the item the same.

— —

SECOND PROTO SAMPLES

If the fit of the samples is really poor and they need a lot of reworking, often a 2nd proto has to be made. This information has to be noted on the development matrix, so the development team doesn't forget about it. This second proto also has to be made, fitted and approved before it can go ahead to the final sample. In some cases, if the factory is efficient and there is a machinist available, it can be made whilst the proto review is in progress. Other times it is made and then sent to the developer around 2 weeks later for approval.

DEVELOPMENT MATRIX – POST PROTO

At this stage of the process, once the fitting has been completed, the development matrix should be a document full of changes and additions. The developer must ensure that it is complete, updated and circulated to the design and the merchandise teams as well as to the factories so that everyone is clear on the sample status.

HANDING OVER

The final part to the review is the recording on the technical pack of all the details made in the fitting. All the separate pages, as mentioned earlier, have to be up to date with the correct colour, fabric, size, branding and fit comments, so that the factory can either make a second proto, or proceed to a salesman sample. The handing over of the updated tech pack is very similar to the handover process at the start of development. It is vitally important to pass on the information in person clearly and in detail. Talk through each point, discussing with the factories whether your ideas are workable, finding solutions for problems and checking and double-checking that they understand what you want and when you want it.

SALESMAN SAMPLE REVIEW

The proto samples, once they have been completed with correct branding, fabrics and fit changes by the factories, become salesman samples, and they are sent from the factories to be reviewed at the offices of the brand for fit, fabric and price ahead of the collection launch.

WHEN DOES IT HAPPEN?

Three weeks before the collection launch the developers, the designers, the merchandiser and the production teams re-fit the key styles (those that best represent the concept idea or are to be used for the look book) to make sure that the finished item is correct for fit and price, and is suitable for launch. This is the first time the production team gets involved, and is seen as a clear handover point from the development team to production.

GARMENTS

During this review the styles selected for the key looks of the concept are fitted, and in some cases amended in length or fit to be closer in mood and shape to the concept, whilst the rest of the range is placed to one side to be reviewed in full at a later stage. In general, all the samples developed and delivered from the factories will be shown at the launch; however, there are always a few styles that don't come through the development process successfully (maybe the colour of the fabric is wrong or the fit of the style is not correct) and these garments are cancelled at the salesman sample review.

It is the production coordinator's responsibility to take notes on all changes or adjustments made during this fitting, as the comments and notes will be crucial for the production tech packs at the later stage of pre production.

PRICES

At the same time as the salesman samples are being reviewed, the final prices, (which are the result of the proto review changes), come through to the developer and the merchandiser. At this stage of the process the final retail prices are discussed between the merchandise, the development and the design teams so that an overall margin (based on the landed, wholesale or retail price) can be set ahead of the launch. These prices are calculated by the merchandiser and entered into the line list, which has already been mentioned in chapter 5. In some cases the prices will be as predicted, while some will be higher. At this point it is too late to make any further design adjustments to alter the price, as the garments have been made, but if there are concerns from the merchandiser regarding profit margins then these are noted and the problem is discussed at the launch preparation, and later at the production fitting stage.

PROFIT MARGIN

A profit margin on a brand's jacket is the proportion of money left over from the sale of the jacket after accounting for its cost price. Essentially, every company wants to make a profit. They have a product at one cost, which they sell at a higher price, and what is left over after all additional costs is the profit.

TARGET PROFIT MARGIN

Generally speaking, most fashion companies work to a target profit margin, which can be anywhere between 45% and 60%. Some product groups will give you a better margin than others, as some garments are more expensive to make while the selling price is more competitive (lower). Overall, a company will try to make a balanced profit margin across all product groups to ensure that in the end they will reach around 50%.

LANDED PRICE

The landed price is the total cost of goods for the manufacture, the freight and insurance up to the port of destination (where the goods are being shipped to). It can also include customs clearance costs and duty (additional costs to bring the goods into the country).

WHOLESALE PRICE

The wholesale price is the price offered to shops that sell the goods. In some cases (depending on the brand) the retail price is 2.6 times the wholesale price. For instance, if a department store wants to buy some clothes from the Tommy Hilfiger range they will pay the wholesale price and then sell it for their own retail price in their store. The wholesale price is higher than the landed price but not as high as the retail price.

INCOTERMS

There is an internationally agreed set of terms for the costs associated with the transportation of goods, called Incoterms. These costs can vary according to who pays for which of the various parts of the process of getting the goods from the factory to the brand's warehouse (e.g. packaging, loading charges, insurance, delivery to the port, export duty, origin terminal charges and loading onto carriage, etc.) and are added by the factory as a percentage of the FOB

cost price to the price charged to the brand. For example, if the total transportation, etc. costs amount to 25% of the FOB price, the manufacturer simply multiplies that by 1.25 as the final cost to the brand. For a Far East country Incoterms may be 1.3 (because there are more costs involved in transportation from the Far East), but for the EU it may be 1.18. These do change on occasion, and are set by the International Chamber of Commerce. Please see the list of useful websites (p. 227) for more information.

TYPES OF MARGINS

There are two types of margin that can be calculated by the merchandiser: a wholesale profit margin and a retail profit margin. If a brand sells to its own shops it would use a retail profit margin to calculate its profit, but if the brand didn't have its own shops, it would sell to others, such as a department store, and in this case the brand would calculate the wholesale profit margin. Both are listed in the example below.

> **Retail profit margin**
> Retail price – landed price / retail price, multiplied by 100

> **Wholesale profit margin**
> Wholesale price - landed price / wholesale price, multiplied by 100

With a brand that sells its goods to another retailer such as a department store, the cost price is actually the landed price (as this is the FOB plus Incoterms), while the selling price is actually the wholesale price. But, if you are selling direct to your own retail shop, then it would be the landed price and the retail-selling price used in the calculation.

COSTING SHEET

SEASON:

FABRICS

	DESCRIPTION	WIDTH	UNIT PR
Cotton Twill (2543)	BODY		12,95
Gingham Check (7104 150 0012	Waistband facing	0	2,50
P777	Along waitband facing	0	5,50
	Full body		2,10

TRIMS

	DESCRIPTION		TOTAL FAB
		SIZE	UNIT PRI
Threads			
Button Ref. 19.915416.13	Inside Waistband		
EHW-63498			
Hanger			
Main label		24	
Size label			
Composition label	THG-100504		
EHW100683	THG-100506		
EHW-57795			
EHW-66020	safety seal		
Zip	Hangerloops		
Metal Tag	Hangtags		
	Centre front		
	Bottom h		

> An example of a costing sheet used by a factory.

EXAMPLE

- -

> A shirt has an actual FOB of 18.64€
> A landed price of 22.00€
  (FOB x Incoterm 1.18)
> A retail price of 129.00€
> A wholesale price of 49.61€
  (retail / 2.6)

The wholesale profit margin is:
49.61€ − 22.00€ / 49.61€ = 55.6%
The retail profit margin is:
129.00€ − 22.00€ / 129.00€ = 83%

You can see that to sell in your own retail stores gives you a better margin than wholesale, but with wholesale you can reach a bigger market. However, it is important to remember that some of the higher profits would need to be spent on building and maintaining your own retail stores, pay the staff, pay all the taxes, etc., so whilst the margin may be higher, there are additional costs involved, which make the difference in margin less favorable.

- -

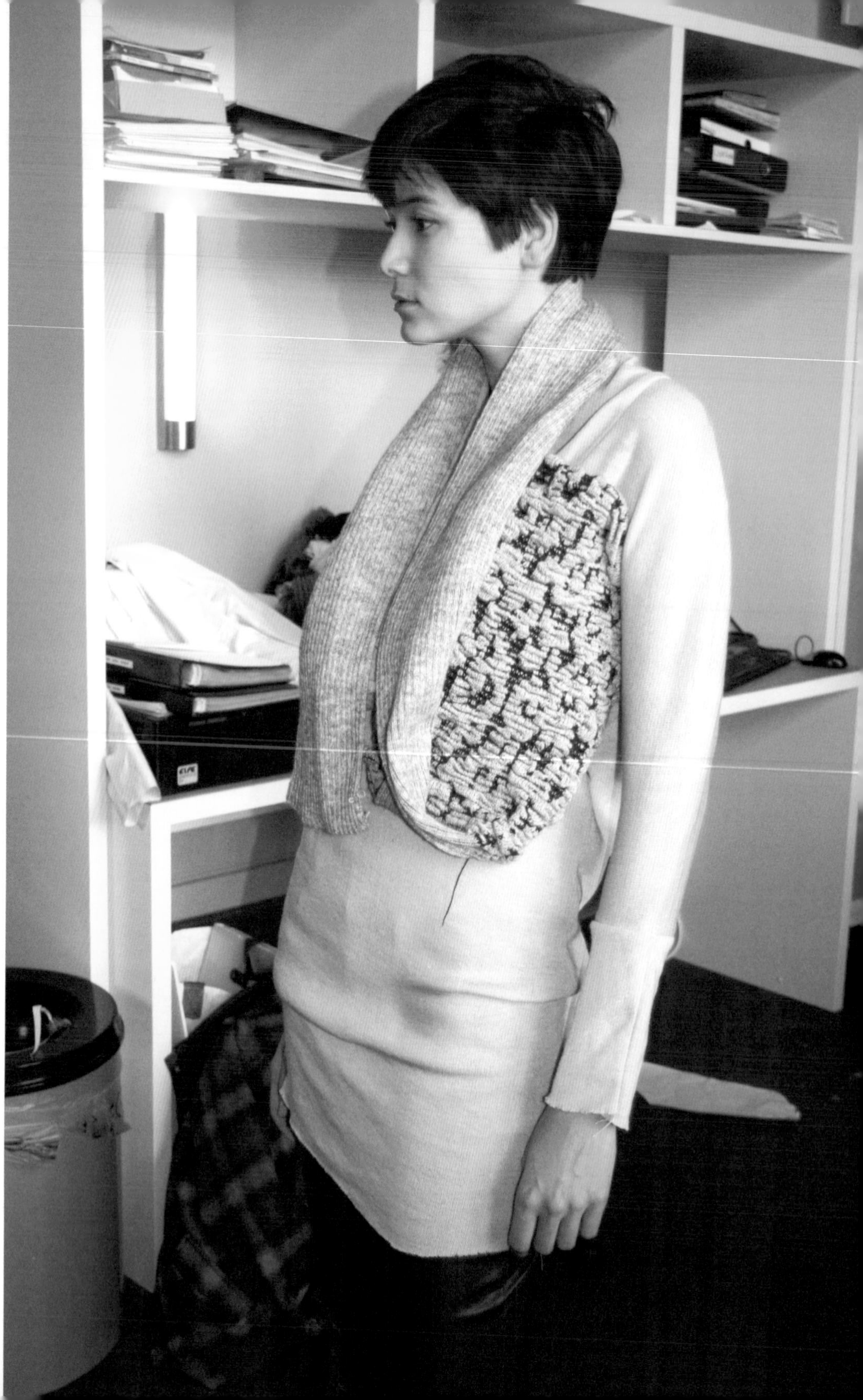

AFTER THE REVIEW

Once this salesman sample review is completed, the cancelled styles are physically removed from the collection and are marked in grey in the line list so it is clear that these styles once existed, but are no longer in the current range. These styles will not be sold. The merchandise team then calculates all the profit margins for the brand based on either a retail profit margin or a wholesale profit margin. This completes the line list, so it is ready for the launch.

PRODUCTION REVIEW

The production review is the final group review within the development and production stages, and includes the designer and the production team. The fit, branding and prices of the collection are reviewed again in the production department of the brand ahead of the start of bulk production.

WHEN DOES IT HAPPEN?

This review can take around two weeks to complete, and happens at the same time as the sales teams are selling the range to their customers. Once the review involving the designer and the production team is finished, the production team updates the technical packs and prepares them for the factories.

GARMENTS

It is very important at the start of production preparation for the production coordinator to measure the garments in order to understand how they compare to the requested size spec. Remember that at the proto review, the development team measured the samples to compare them to the specifications that had been requested. Now the production team follows the same process ahead of the production fitting. From these measurements

they are in a better position to judge the garment when fitted.

FIT CONTINUITY

It may be a really obvious point to make at this stage, but by using the same fit model throughout the development and production process means that you have continuity in fit and changes to measurements are kept to a minimum.

Always check the fit model's proportions. Two models can be the same dress size, but one may be much taller than the other. Fitting a dress on the taller model will bring implications to body length that may not have been experienced in the first fit. Proportionally, the waist will be in the same position on the dress but the waist of the dress will sit on a different position on a taller model compared to the shorter; additionally, the sleeve length may be different and the skirt length will also vary. Making changes at the production fit to compensate for these differences will have implications to the shorter person should they refit the dress. This is not to say that changes can't be made if you use two different models, but it is definitely something you have to take into consideration.

PRODUCTION FITTING

Preparing yourself for the production fitting is not so different from what needed to be done for the proto fitting, only now you will have the finished garment in the correct fabric, colour and branding. Be prepared with the technical packs, the line list, the fabric and trim files, and any additional notes taken at the salesman sample review. Additionally, you should also have available any comments that were made about the garment during the line launch meetings

P/P
pre-production
red seal

Only one sample made of each style
Made in either salesman or bulk fabric
May not have all labels and branding
May have fit and style alterations
May also be an existing style in new fabric
Made in sample size
Needs to be fitted and comments made

s/s
size set
red seal

One of each size made (up to 10 samples depending on size scale)
Made in either salesman or bulk fabric
Usually sent if there are key aspects that need to be proportional
May have fit and style alterations
Needs to be fitted and comments made
At least one needs to be in sample size
Should have all branding and labels attached

bulk / shipping
sample
gold seal

One sample is taken from bulk shipment
Will be in actual bulk fabric
Will have all branding and final labels attached
Will have been made according to the comments of P/P or s/s
Will be in sample size so it can be compared to selling sample
This should be fitted and approved so that the shipment can be made

Sometimes the sales teams give feedback on the fit of the garments. These comments made by the sales teams should be made known to the production team at this fitting. It is very important for the production team to physically see the garment on when discussing these comments, as only then can essential changes be made and measurements corrected.

PRE-PRODUCTION SAMPLES
During the production fitting, the production team and pattern maker analyse the fit and make of the salesman sample. If the fit is not correct, or perhaps the sales teams have made suggestions for changing the style, it is common for another sample to be requested by the team. This sample is called a pre-production sample (PP sample) and needs to be approved by both the production team and the pattern maker before production can start.

© Sandy Chiu

It is made in the correct fabric with correct branding and should be a true representation of what the produced garments will be like when in the stores.

SIZE SET

Another type that is sometimes requested is a size set of samples, which is a set of three or more samples of the same style but in the different sizes that will be ordered. This is requested by the brand when it is important to see how the different sizes within the style affect the proportions of the style. Perhaps a style includes large pockets; if you use the same size pocket for a s as is used on an xl the proportions will look strange, so something called grading is used, and a full size set for a style will give a true representation of all the sizes of the pockets.

Sometimes, however, a size set is requested for a style that has a greater size coverage, for instance denim. If jeans are made in a size scale starting with 23" and ending in 36", this will include the sizes 23, 24, 25, 26, 27, 28, 29, 30, 32, 34, and 36. As denim is nearly

always washed, which can have strange effects on shrinkage, it is necessary to get full or half size sets to check all proportions and measurements. A full size set in denim would include all the sizes, but a half may have 24, 26, 28 and 30. Some brands request a full size set for every style and some only for select styles.

In the diagrams above you can see that proportions in a garment play a huge part in the size spec, and because of that, for some styles we ask for a size set to ensure that the proportions look correct for all the sizes. On the three sketches we see that three sizes are involved: xs, s and m. On the sketches the same size pockets and belt have been used for all sizes so you can see that where it is correct proportionally for the xs, they are much too small for the m. The pockets and belt should be graded up proportionally to avoid this.

GRADING OR GRADE RULE

When the production teams have fitted all the samples and are updating the technical

Julie Dress / Proto No. W124-12 / Composition: 100% Silk						
	Size XS	Size S	Size M	Size L	Size XL	Grade	Tolerance
---	---	---	---	---	---	---	---
Front body length from HSP	37 1/4	38	38 3/4	39 1/2	40 1/4	3/4	3/8
Back body length from CB	34 1/4	35	35 3/4	36 1/2	37 1/4	3/4	3/8
Shoulder slope		0					1/8
Shoulder seam	3 1/2	3 1/2	3 1/2	3 1/2	3 1/2		1/8
Shoulder width	12 3/4	13 1/4	13 3/4	14 1/4	14 3/4	1/2	1/4
Cross front (- 4 1/2" down from CB)	- 3/4	0	3/4	1 1/2	2 1/4	3/4	3/8
Cross back (- 4 1/2" down from CB)	- 3/4	0	3/4	1 1/2	2 1/4	3/4	3/8

packs for the factories, they will make a graded spec for the style. This is what the factory uses for production. Grading or a grade rule is the difference between sizes. There are very specific rules applied that pattern makers follow when they are making patterns. For example, sometimes on the chest size of a T-shirt the difference between sizes may be 1". This is called the grade rule for the chest. Each location on a garment has a set of rules, which also vary between brands.

Once the production manager makes this decision as to which new samples have to be made, the information is added to the production-planning sheet, which will later be sent to the factories so they can begin their internal planning (see chapter 5). On some occasions, where the fit of the style is poor, a new pattern will need to be made. In this case the pattern maker is informed and the new pattern is sent with the technical pack to the factory.

BRANDING

At this stage all of the branding will have been added and confirmed, but sometimes there are comments from the sales meetings that result in requests for branding to be added to specific styles. This additional branding is dealt with here and is added to the technical packs by the production team.

PRICES

I have already explained at the start of this section that the production fitting takes place at the same time as the collection is being sold by the sales teams. As a result, the merchandise teams are beginning to receive weekly sales updates, including sales quantities from all the markets. The merchandiser adds this information to the line list, so that she can start to create weighted profit margins for the collection, which in turn can produce financial reports for the brand.

WEIGHTED PROFIT MARGIN

Calculation of a weighted profit margin includes the number of pieces in that style that have been sold, so it is a more accurate indication of the contribution the style makes towards the profitability of the collection. Once the orders have been made, the weighted margin is calculated for each

A basic price shirt

A basic shirt style with an FOB of 21.00€ and a RRP of 129.00€, has a margin of 50% and has projected sales of 900 pieces.

FOB: 21.00€

Landed price: 21.00€ x 1.18 (Incoterm) = 24.78€
(in total value 24.78€ x 900 pieces = 22 302€)

Wholesale price: 129.00€ / 2.6 = 49.61€
(in total value 49.61€ x 900 pieces = 44 649€)

Margin: 44 649€ - 22 302€ / 44 649€ % = 50%

A top price shirt

A top price style with an FOB of 30.00€ and a RRP of 149.00€, has a margin of 38% and has projected sales of 3000 pieces.

FOB: 30.00€

Landed price: 30.00€ x 1.18 (Incoterm) = 35.40€
(in total value 35.40€ x 3000 pieces = 106 200€)

Wholesale price: 149.00€ / 2.6 = 57.30€
(in total value 57.30€ x 3000 pieces = 171 900€)

Margin: 171 900€ - 106 200€ / 171 900€ % = 38%

style and analysed by the merchandiser to give a more accurate indication of the final profit margin after sales. How does this work? I'll recap here the pricing information:

> **The FOB is the final price of the garment as sent from the factory.**
> **The landed price is the FOB price combined with the special shipping costs associated with the country of manufacture.**
> **The wholesale price is the retail price minus the mark up.**
> **The margin is the % of profit for each style.**

The calculation of the weighted profit margin is: total wholesale value – total landed value / total wholesale value, multiplied by 100.

In the example above you can see the calculation of the weighted profit margin for a basic style and a top style shirt. The basic shirt has a lower wholesale value but higher profit margin (50%) than the higher price shirt, which only has a

margin of 38%. In fact, the higher price shirt will drag down the overall margin to just 40% if you take an average. On the other hand, while the percentage profit may be lower on it, the brand will make almost three times as much money (65 700€ against 22 347€) on the top style shirt (22€ profit per shirt) because it sells better than the basic style (25€ profit per shirt). So, the merchandisers have to weigh the benefit of higher sales volumes against the 'cost' of lower profit margins. Many companies made their fortunes on just such calculations.

AFTER THE REVIEW

To fit a whole range of samples for production can take the team anything up to two weeks, depending on the size of the range. The next step for the production team following the fitting is to collate all the updated information onto the technical packs ready to hand over to the factories. As with all the stages mentioned so far, a face-to-face handover at the factory means a more effective transfer of information and a smoother production process.

- -

Reviews are opportunities to assess the range at key
stages. Everyone will have an opinion; step back, take
notes and accept that it will be a busy and confusing
few days.

The key to a successful review is preparation. There is
no excuse for not having all your files, sketches, fabrics
and colours with you.

Take copious amounts of notes, and once the review is
over, make a clear summary or all decisions and circulate
it to everyone who was there. People do forget.

Always take pictures of the garments. Visual aids are
better than a style number or a rushed description.

Having a good relationship with the factory, agent or
buying office will make the review easier when it comes
to finding last minute solutions to changes and additions.

- -

Style: Big cuff pants
Article nr.: 90110
Size: 38, 40, 42
Price: 96/240

Catelijn

Style: Triangle pants
Article nr.: 90210
Size: 38, 40, 42
Price: 104/260

Steffi

Selina

Style: Double waistband pants
Article nr.: 90512
Size: 38, 40, 42

Doortje

Style: Wide leg trousers
Article nr.: 90611
Size: 38, 40, 42
Price: 100/250

IX

Chapter 9: **Launching & Sales**

The launch of a collection follows a development period of between three and nine months, and is the first time the whole collection will be seen by the design, development, merchandising and production teams in its final form with the fabrics, colours and fit, hopefully, as the designer originally envisaged. The method of launch can mean anything from a rail of garments displayed in an apartment to a catwalk show at an international fashion week, but regardless of the method of launch, the sole purpose is to sell the styles to get the production orders for the styles which will be made by different factories and shipped to the stores to be bought by the end consumer.

TYPES OF LAUNCHES

There are many different methods of launching a range, a private view in a showroom, a catwalk show, an internet live stream, a shop opening, an inter-company meeting and a trade show. Most brands these days have both catwalk and inter-company launches; catwalk shows being purely for PR, whilst the inter-company launch is sales driven. For our examples we shall look at a catwalk show, an inter company sales launch and a trade show.

CATWALK SHOWS

Catwalk shows at the international fashion weeks are held twice a year at major hubs around the world, and are attended by the international fashion press, fashion buyers from large and small retail stores and celebrities. Most main cities have their own fashion weeks to showcase international and local talent, but the main ones publicised in the press are: New York, London, Paris and Milan. A catwalk show can last from five to twenty minutes and shows models walking down a catwalk with outfits that have been styled by the brand's creative team. There are

no displays showing concept boards or rails of clothes. Instead, it is a slick production costing thousands of Euros /dollars.

INTER-COMPANY LAUNCHES

An inter-company sales launch is an in house meeting comprising the sales teams, designers, developers, merchandisers and the production team, meeting usually in a separate venue, away from the brand's office, for up to a week. The concept, garments,

colours and prices are reviewed for each market, and workshops relating to selling techniques, pricing and styling are offered to train the salesmen to enhance the sales.

INDUSTRY TRADE SHOWS

Trade shows have been used for many years as a method of showcasing your brand. These are a great source of inspiration and trend validation, as looking at other people's collections and gaining a new perspective

TRUE STORY

I worked for a brand that had an external design/development team, and for the first season we had an extremely short development time frame. As we moved closer to the launch date we found it harder and harder to get exact product information from the external team, and we started to get concerned. With one month to go before the launch we still hadn't

set up styles in the system, create a line book and manage the pricing set up for sales.

Exactly one week before launching we received the garments and were at last able to put together all the selling tools needed to launch this new brand. We managed in seven days what most teams do in three months.

Preparation time	6 months
Presentation time	15 minutes
Location	Venue at Fashion Week
Purpose	Press and buying presentation
Details	Celebrity driven / Buying starts 2 days later / Garments shown on models

Catwalk

Preparation time	6 months
Presentation time	1 week
Location	Private venue or within company office
Purpose	Launch for company sales teams and offices
Details	No press involved directly / No celebrity presence / Sales start approx 1 week later / Selling workshops are given to aid sales and range understanding / Each piece is shown individually, but key looks are merchandised

Wholesale

Preparation time	6 months
Presentation time	1 week
Location	Private venue or within company office
Purpose	Launch for company sales teams and offices
Details	No press involved directly / No celebrity presence / Sales start approx 1 week later / Pieces and looks are merchandised in shop fit mock-ups within the company building and then replicated around their stores / The capsules of the ranges are designed to be merchandised by colour so it's important to show them this way

Retail

on your own, is a useful tool. Bread&Butter in Berlin, Pitti Uomo in Florence and Magic in Las Vegas are just a few examples of international events, but there are just as many local fashion weeks in which you can rent a space and show the range to local and international buyers and retailers. If you are a small brand, launching it is a great opportunity to reach out to customers, but also to catch up with existing ones. They can, however, be expensive to fund and there is more of a trend now to use online methods for brand promotion, leaving the large trade shows for the big corporate companies. Larger brands use these shows as a PR exercise, staging catwalk shows and special events to gain brand awareness.

Waiting for a catwalk show
at Amsterdam Fashion Week.

TRUE STORY

The first time I was involved on a catwalk line, I started the day after the show and there were no clear notes as to which styles had been used. Of course you can see online the runway shows, so in some cases it was clear about the jackets and coats but not for the items underneath which were still marginally visible (vests, shirts). Trying to list all the garments from a website picture is complicated. The following season I was at the show and witnessed over a hundred changes of style, garments and running order before the show, so rather than panic with pen and paper, I sat back, embraced the surreal and insanely exciting experience of a catwalk show and the morning after the show I went through the rails where all the garments were hanging for all the individual 'looks', making all the notes I needed.

Style: Roll sleeve dress
Article nr : 90260EC
Size: 38, 40, 42
Price: 142/330

Style: Closed blouse
Article nr : 90130EC
Size: 38, 40, 42
Price: 45/119

SELLING TOOLS

A selling tool is a document or series of documents, which help the sales teams sell the collection to their customers. The first one, mentioned in chapter 5, is the line list, which is an information-rich, financial document created by the merchandise team. The other two, frequently used by many brands, are a look book and a line book.

THE LOOK BOOK

A look book contains photographs of models wearing outfits selected by the design and merchandise teams from the collection, which best encapsulate the brand's concept for that season (see chapter 2). Shooting the look book is an expensive process, but it is an investment for the brand, as the photos are used not only by the sales teams for showroom styling, but also as visual aids to drive the sales. With the look books sometimes uploaded and used on mobile (internet) devices, they can also be shared for use on customer's e-commerce sites where actual photographs are required.

THE LINE BOOK

Line books, put together by the designer, are visual representations of the merchandisers' line list and consist of CAD (computer aided design) drawings, fabric, colour offer and price information. A cheaper alternative than a look book, the line books can take up to four weeks to produce, and are vital selling tools when it comes to launching the collection. If any of this information is not correct, the sales cannot be recorded and the styles will not be produced.

Key aspects of the line book are:

> **Style name**
> **Fabric name**
>   (waxy cotton, drapey wool)
> **Fabric composition**
>   (100% cotton)
> **Colour names**
>   ('perfect pink' or 'sunny yellow')
> **Sizes available for sales**
>   (XS, S, M, L, XL)
> **Coloured up sketches**
> **Barcode for scanning and
>   recording orders**
> **Price** (cost and retail)
> **Delivery drop**

COLOUR OFFER

The colour offer mentioned in the line book is simply the range of colours in which the style can be bought. As we have seen through the earlier stages, when the designers create a style and select the fabric, they also have a colour palette they work with. These colours derive from the concept and change each season. Not every style can be sampled in every shade (as this would be too expensive for the brand) but what the design/development team can do is to make a colour offer for each style, enabling the customer to buy the style (seen on the catwalk on the mannequin) in a variety of colours. These sketches are shown in a line book each season. This saves money for the company and increases sales.

MAKING THE SELLING TOOLS

The selling tools are compiled during the four-week period leading up the collection launch. Made by the design and the merchandise teams, it is another example of teams working together to maintain the flow of information.

SALES

The sales team of any brand is there to sell the collection to their customers, who can mean either a large department store or a small independent store, but not to the general public. Each brand has a range of countries where it sells, such as France, Germany and Spain, and these are called the sales markets. Each sales market will have its own sales office, which has a set of the salesman samples and a sales team who try to identify new stores to sell the brand to. When they find a new store or customer, they invite them to the sales office and show them the new collection.

ABCD FORECASTING

Some companies call it A, B, C, D and some 1, 2, 3, 4, but whichever the term, on the last day of the launch, the sales teams work through the line list and the garments adding a number or letter, making a forecast for the merchandise team so that the range can be reduced in size before sales appointments begin. A or 1 is a best seller, D or 4 is for a worst seller. Forecasting means looking at the appropriateness of each style to the range and to their local sales market, predicting which styles will be successful and will generate a large production order and which should be cancelled. It can also be used as an indication for pre booking fabrics. All styles that receive a majority bottom grade are taken out of the range and the remaining styles are open for sales. This reduces the size of the range considerably, and makes it more focused for the individual sales markets. Once this forecast has been made, the launch is over, and the sale teams begin selling to their local customers.

ORDER FORECASTING

Order forecasting is also used throughout the sales period to give indications of quantities for each style. With the sales underway, the merchandise teams can ask for weekly or fortnightly forecasts on sales figures to help in the production planning.

SELLING THE RANGE

Before the sales agents start selling the range they meet with their customers, sometimes a few weeks prior to launch, so as to gain an appreciation of the customers' budgets for that season. Knowledge of this budget enables the sales agent to focus the sales meeting towards what the customer is likely to want and can afford. There is usually a fixed period allowed for selling the collection, which can be 2 to 8 weeks, and during that time the sales team members make sales appointments with the regular customers and also with new ones. As the role of the sales team is to sell the collection, it is important for them and for the brand to expand the network of customers every season. The customer may place an order for some of the collection, and this order at the end of the day will be sent to the merchandise team of the brand. After the selling period, all the customer orders are collated and this becomes the production quantity.

SALES COMMENTS

During the launch of a collection, including the forecast, and throughout the selling period, the sales teams look at the collection using their local market experience and sometimes make requests to cancel, add or change styles to make their collection more country specific. The merchandising, design and production teams assess the viability of the local requests within the collection and if they are agreed, the changes are publicised in a newsletter or sales memo.

The merchandising team sends these to the sales, production and design teams to update them on the changes or cancellations arising from the local market requests. The newsletters take the form of emails, Excel charts or Word documents, and are sent at least twice a week within the selling timelines.

CANCELLED STYLES

Cancellations to styles have bigger implications than just greying a line in the line list. Cancelling a style requires the merchandising team to rebalance the range plan, ensuring there are enough items per product group and per fabric and colour to reach the sales target or to satisfy the sales teams' demands. I have mentioned in chapter 4 that there are minimum quantities attached to fabrics for production. If in a collection you have one colour of fabric being used for two styles, and one of those styles is cancelled, the fabric mill or factory needs to confirm to the production team that it can still meet the minimums for the remaining style.

ADDING STYLES

It is always possible to add styles into the range at this stage of the process, provided they are a justified addition. If there is a genuine gap in the range for style, colour or fabric, then the style can be added if the forecast sales are high enough and there is fabric available. If the request is for a style from a previous season then the decision needs careful consideration. The collection is there to create newness in the market and resurrecting previous seasons' styles is not always the way to go. If the style is a basic one and can be added into one of this season's fabrics and colours, then there are possibilities. In such a case, the merchandise team usually requests that the sales teams provide a sales figure for each of the additions so as to make sure it is financially viable.

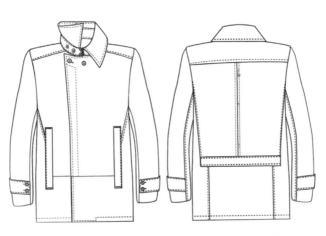

Overston Coat

112EH-C007-F311S-N001

Black

100% Wool / Leather

112EH-C007U-F311S-N001

Black (not sampled)

100% Wool

112EH-C007U-F316S-R002

Red / Black

100% Wool

112EH-C007U-F313S-V003

Green

100% Wool

112EH-C007U-F309S-G002

Grey

100% Wool

Example of a linebook page with the sketch, colour pieces and fabric compositions.

SHOULDER PADS
DEFINE TAILORING

ASSYMETRIC
COLLAR WITH
ZIP TO OPEN
ONE SIDE OF
COLLAR

LOOSE SLEEVES

CONTRAST COLOUR
UNDER SIDE
OF BELT &
LINING

DB COAT

- HALF LINED

- DB CLOSURE,
SB BOTTOM SECTION

- POCKETS ON SIDE
SEAMS

Designers' illustrations are sometimes
used as selling tools because they bring
flat sketches to life.

This sales figure from the sales team needs to be workable for the factories' production and fabric minimums; if these are both acceptable, then the style or colour can be added. If only one sales team has requested this added style and it doesn't reach the fabric minimums then the merchandisers will make this request open to all the sales teams in all the markets to see if they want to add to their sales figures as well. This sometimes helps to increase the expected sales, and it can make the style addition possible. Once the quantities are known, the merchandise team will issue a purchase order and the style will be added to the line list.

CHANGES TO STYLES

Style changes, or design updates, can be anything from removing a pocket to adding sleeves, and are much easier to handle than style additions. The changes are usually handled by the production team and are worked into the fitting comments for production. Changes to styles during the sales period are an additional part of the production process, and easy to manage for the production team and the factory. All changes, however, have implications for the price, so new prices need to be calculated by the factory, sent to the merchandise team and entered into the line list.

Reviewing the pricing is a complicated and time-consuming process involving the merchandise and the production teams and the manufacturer. The final prices that were entered into the line list for the launch are in some cases subject to change as styles are amended, updated or added. As a result, there is a continuing dialogue between the above teams on whether to maintain the profit margin or the target prices, or to establish new prices following the changes.

BULK ORDERS

Throughout the sales period the sales teams enter all their order quantities from the sales meetings, the merchandise team collates all the figures and analyses the bulk orders per style, colour and size. These will eventually be the basis of a purchase order.

At this stage the merchandiser and the production teams decide if the buy quantity/purchase order should include a stock quantity as well, or whether it should be exactly what was ordered. If a style has great potential within the range then the order should include some extra stock, which can be over and above the actual sales figures. This stock can be used for replenishment if the style sells out in the stores. If no additional stock is ordered, that shows less confidence in a style and that the brand will be happy to sell the amount ordered and no more.

The decision about stock quantities may have very important consequences for the profitability of the range, because sometimes these styles turn out to be a huge success, but if there is no additional stock, it means that once they are sold out, that is it. If the fabric has a short production lead time, then the factory can remake the style in about two months, but if the fabric has a long lead time, the chance of reordering the style is slight and it will not be possible to replenish the stores with that style before the end of the season. On the other hand, ordering and holding reserve stock in a style that is less successful can be an expensive mistake.

MERCHANDISE PLANNING

Merchandise planning is managed by the merchandise and the production teams and involves a complicated planning process whereby the fabrics, colours and buy quantities are coordinated to ensure that everyone (factories, fabric mills, sales teams and merchandising) obtain a workable order.

Let's take a look at a fictional shirts range, at the role of merchandising and at the fabrics used. In the image below, you will see that four fabrics are selected: basic poplin, stretch poplin, poplin stripe and check poplin. You can also see the comparison between the fabric minimums by style, colour and quantity. Basic and stretch poplin fabrics have minimum quantities required by fabric style, which means that it doesn't matter how many colours you have, it is the total quantity of fabric altogether that matters (see chapter 4). The poplin stripe and poplin check, however, have minimums by colour, which is tougher to achieve, as you have to have high sales in specific colours to keep the styles in the production schedule.

Traditionally, solid colours in fabrics are sold in greater quantities than checks and stripes, so from an early stage you should be concerned about how this combination of stripes and checks will work for production. If we know the minimums for the fabrics and also the average requirement of fabric used for a shirt, we can establish the number of shirts needed per fabric and from here we can make a comparison to the order quantities.

Basic poplin

Fabric minimums: 500 m per quality
Requirement for a shirt: 1.3 m
No. of shirts per fabric minimum:
approximately 385 shirts per fabric quality
Total Buy: 850 shirts
Result: No difficulty in meeting the minimums

Stretch poplin

Fabric minimums: 500 m per quality
Requirement for a shirt: 1.3 m
No. of shirts per fabric:
approximately 385 shirts per fabric quality
Total buy: 1970 shirts
Result: No difficulty in meeting the minimums

Poplin stripe

Fabric minimums: 800 m per colour
Requirement for a shirt: 1.3 m
No. of shirts per fabric:
approximately 615 shirts per fabric colour
Total buy: 300 shirts in red, 100 shirts in green
Result: unable to reach colour minimums

Check poplin

Fabric minimums: 800 m per colour
Requirement for a shirt: 1.3 m
No. of shirts per fabric:
approximately 615 shirts per fabric colour
Total buy: 150 green shirts, 200 shirts in blue
Result: unable to reach colour minimums

OPTIONS

The first thing to mention before we look at the options in this situation is that choosing a fabric that has such high minimums as 800 m per colour is a very unwise move. This should never have been chosen at the development stage. The fact that it was means that the production team has to find a solution so as to keep both of the check and the stripe fabrics in the range.

As you can see from the examples below, there are many possible ways to solve a problem like this, and ultimately, it involves every part of the team.

> **Checking with the fabric mills**
You can check with the fabric mill to see if they have a similar fabric, with maybe a different composition and lower minimums, which can be used instead.

> **Checking with all the sales markets**
The merchandising team can contact all the markets again and ask them to recheck their budget to see if they can buy a few extra pieces to increase the buy quantity as a whole.

> **Increase the buy**
The sales team can increase the order quantity for both of the colour ways to reach the minimums; however, there will be a large quantity of spare stock available. This would have financial implications for the brand later on when the style is put on sale.

> **Cancel the colours**
The merchandise team can cancel the colours of the check and stripe completely, which solves the problem of the high minimums, but at the same time would make the range much less fashionable. The sales teams will have to re-balance their orders to ensure that the customers receive a balanced range in terms of colour. Maybe one of the colours can be cancelled and the remaining ones be increased to reach the minimums; this way we keep the range fashionable.

> **Adding a style**
The design team can take an existing basic style and re-fabricate with the check or the stripe. They know that the style works in a basic fabric, so they can add another dimension to the range by adding it in a patterned fabric.

SOLUTIONS

Possible solutions in this scenario are:

> **The solution for the poplin stripe:**
'Style Charlie' in the green stripe is cancelled. 'Style Andrew' is added in the red stripe with a buy of 250 pieces, which takes the total buy to 550 shirts.

For the balance of the fabric you can take on the liability (meaning you have left over fabric which you have to pay for).

> **The solution for the check poplin:**
The fabric mill has suggests to change the base to a cotton / polyester instead of 100% cotton. You can use one of their own check designs, which is very similar, and as they have stock available, you can meet their minimums.

176

DELIVERY DATES

Now that the merchandise team has
finalized the production planning, they
begin to prepare the bulk purchase orders
for the factories. One of the most important
pieces of information to be included in the
purchase order, is the delivery date or ex
factory date. The delivery date is actually
factored into the planning, in some cases at
an early stage during the sales period, but
as it is dependent on the end order quantity,
it remains an expectation until the bulk order
is finalized. The merchandisers' planning has
not only to make sure that the orders meet
fabric minimums, but also that the date the
purchase orders are delivered to the shops is
also acceptable.

THEMES, HITS OR DROPS

Some brands divide the delivery of their
stock to stores into the themes or colour
blocks relating to the concept. Perhaps
the blues will be first, followed by the reds
and then the greens. What this essentially
means is that the customer sees a flow of
new product every two months, giving them
a reason to revisit the store and buy more
items. These different sections of the range
are known as themes, 'hits' or 'drops'.

PURCHASE ORDERS

A purchase order, or PO, is an official and
legally binding order document created by
the brand, in this case represented by the
merchandise team, to place an order with
a factory. It includes the style information,
payments details, shipping information, final

New season's collections in store.

price, and order quantity split into size and colour. The other crucial element in the PO is the delivery date required by the brand.

The factory cannot confirm a final delivery date without a final order quantity, which in turn cannot be confirmed until sales are over. The PO's are based on information from the line list, and a member of the merchandise team creates them. The PO is officially placed into the production planning once the factory has received this.

There are several different terms used to describe the delivery dates in the delivery process. Using the correct terms for delivery date and bulk shipment date is imperative, as different aspects of the process use different terms. To use the terms below incorrectly can cause serious misunderstanding:

> ### Ex factory / bulk shipment date
This means when the goods leave the factory. You can also use bulk shipment date, but an exact description of the process should be ex-factory date.

> ### Delivery date 'to forwarder', 'to warehouse' or 'to shop'
The delivery date needs to be specified further, according to whether it is to the warehouse, the forwarder or the shop, Simply using a 'delivery date' is too vague for the factory and can mean several things, which could vary by up to 4 weeks, so it is important to be exact.

> ### In store date
The date the goods reach the store that sells directly to the end customer.

> ### ETD
This can mean Estimated Time of Delivery or Estimated Time of Departure, so be precise in its use. The important thing to remember is that there isn't a right or wrong set of terms, they just need to be agreed by both the merchandisers and the factory. If you are establishing a code of terms or abbreviations, be clear with your team as to what you will be using, so that there are no misunderstandings.

DELIVERY TIME SCALES

The way to calculate the transport time of your order is to start with a date you need the goods in store and work backwards to achieve the ex factory date. These time scales need to be calculated by the merchandising team and specified on the PO, which is sent to the factory. Only then can production begin.

STOCK POSITION

With the factories production process in flow and completed orders being shipped from the factories to the brand's warehouse, the merchandise team track the stock position to establish which PO-s are in the stores and which are still to be delivered. If some orders are late from the factory, the merchandise team will make the decision as to whether the mode of transport for the order can be changed in order to speed up the delivery. If the goods are coming from overseas, the shipment method can change from sea to air, but if the goods are made closer to home, there is little that can be done to speed up the process.

SALES ANALYSIS

The final aspect of the role of the merchandise team is the collating of the sales figures once the production has been shipped to the stores and the true sales with the end customer begins. Analysing the colour, shape, product group and manufacturers performance can be used immediately for the new season's preparation.

For the developer, launching a range is the end of the season. For the production team it is the start. A launch is always a mix of exhaustion and fresh energy.

Watching the catwalk show of a collection you have spent 6 months having sleepless nights over, is one of the most validating experiences as a developer.

The sales teams are there to sell the collection, and as a result will have different views on what's right and wrong for the range. Their opinion is just as valid as yours.

179

Merchandise planning is complicated and time consuming, but essential to a successful production. Learn to be flexible; try to understand the priorities of others in the overall process. The merchandise team will expect you to bring solutions to the table.

In production, be very clear about the use of dates and shipping terms with the factories. Don't let a delay of four weeks result from a miscommunicated delivery date or term.

Chapter 10: **The Future**

Policies, such as corporate responsibility, sustainability, compliance, and supply chain management, were relatively unheard of 20 years ago. But the mere mention of them in the fashion workplace now will invite a wide range of opinions relating to recycling, bottlenecks and local community initiatives. The question is are they only relevant to large corporate businesses or it something even fledgling entrepreneurs can and need to consider? Within this chapter we take a look at what these ideas mean and how they are all co-dependent. I'll look at how each term can be understood for all business levels, and why they are so important to the future of the industry.

CORPORATE RESPONSIBILITY

Corporate responsibility (CR) is a self-regulating record set by businesses to ensure that they adhere to and maintain the ethical standards the international industry sets as its norms.

For instance, if a company prides itself on insisting that its factories pay above the minimum wage, it needs to ensure it keeps to its declared policy. If it advertises this fact on its website, but then defaults and doesn't audit its factories, it is failing in its CR. Regular assessment checks by the brand should ensure that the CR requirements are observed. Some experts also see it as the umbrella term covering social responsibility and sustainability.

SUSTAINABILITY

According to *The World Charter*, the aim of sustainability is to achieve "a sustainable global society founded on respect for nature, universal human rights, economic justice, and a culture of peace." This term has been a key phrase over the last few years, especially since Al Gore's 2006 film *An Inconvenient Truth*, and while it is easy to think that it is just the use of resources and of raw materials that need to be sustained, it is often forgotten that changing the corporate mentality is equally important.

COMPLIANCE

Compliance or 'social responsibility' is, in effect, conforming to a rule, such as a specification, law or standard. In this case, if there is a law applied to employee minimum age or a standard for health and safety, compliance checks ensure that they are observed. Audits, now more commonly known as 'assessments', are carried regularly (in some cases every few weeks) to ensure that the standards are met and any new measure related to the worker, factory or economy is managed carefully and in the correct manner.

Many brands see these assessments as collaborations with the factories to create action plans to aid what is known as capacity building (which is strengthening the skills and abilities of people to enhance the companies' development). By understanding the obstacles that hinder the manufacturers' development, the brand's capacity action plan will allow the manufacturer to achieve greater results in all areas of their business.

SMALL STEPS FORWARD

Initial small steps by individuals can set examples and assist the greater goal, especially, when undertaken from within the corporate giants of the industry. Companies, such as MADE-BY (*www.made-by.org*), are non profit organisations (NPO-s) who work alongside brands and clothing companies large and small as support or 'change agents', giving the brands the tools and knowledge to solve problems themselves that arise from their manufacturing queries. Finding solutions through projects initiated by the brand and by the NPO-s can enable alternative fabric selections, dyeing techniques and washing facilities, all of which can have major implications for environmental considerations, time, pricing, and also for long term resource demands. By setting small, project-based assignments, companies like MADE-BY are tackling the issues at ground level, and teaching a whole new generation of developers to embrace new ideas and new ways of working.

© Amsterdam Fashion Institute, Individuals, Spring/Summer '09

Yarns to be woven into fabric;
just one phase of a supply chain.

REALISTIC EXPECTATIONS

Most brands are realistic in their
expectations. Whilst it is possible to have
an eco cotton T-shirt with a vegetable-based
dye, made locally and transported by bike
to the stores, it is not realistic to expect this
to work on a larger scale. Instead, brands
establish their end objectives and manage
the process accordingly. Some companies
may move all their production from the Far
East to Europe, which reduces their carbon
footprint on transportation. They may also
insist that the washhouses that make their
denims use water-recycling facilities, or that
the hangtags for the denims are made from
recycled card. Other steps could include
reinforcing the same disciplines and ideals
within their own head offices. Recycling
waste paper is enforced, shutting down
computers rather than leaving them on
standby is encouraged, and lights remain off
in an empty office. Even the most simple and
obvious changes can make a difference to
a company's contribution to sustainability.

SUPPLY CHAIN MANAGEMENT

Supply chain management (SCM) can be
seen as a by-product of CR, and is about
managing a network of processes to provide
the end customer with a valued package
(better price/quality). However, it is not
purely about achieving the best margin or
lowest price, it is also about building and
maintaining long term relationships with
everyone involved, in order to get better
products and better deliveries in the long
term. Regular performance reviews are
undertaken between supplier (factory, trim
maker, or fabric mill) and client (brand) to set
goals with a view to improve both the quality
of the partnerships and of the finished
product.

Everyone is working towards a unified goal – the successful production of a garment, and each stage needs to run smoothly and without delay. By evaluating the processes involved right through from fabric buying and button development to manufacturing and transportation, the problematic bottlenecks are removed in the chain to improve communication, work flow and business relationships. Ensuring that brands use partners who share the same principles for all these processes is costly in time and money, but it is essential to the reputation of the company.

MANAGING COMMUNICATION

Remember also that scm is not only about the manufacturing process, it is about the workplace of the brand as well. There are many internal processes, which, if not adhered to, can cause delays in the information flow. Managing the process and communication inside the team is just as important as outside the company. With so much of the development and production process ruled by time lines, it makes the evaluation of these goals easy to assess and monitor. Lack of clarity about roles and responsibilities means a duplication of some procedures and the omission of others, which is inefficient. Giving people clear goals, challenging roles and achievable targets makes the shared task achievable, and will have a positive effect on the quality and accuracy of the information leaving the company. Additionally, if there are not enough people in a team, important tasks may be rushed, ignored or managed badly. Looking back at the roles described in chapter 1 can help you to build an effective team of key players.

RESPONSIBILITY OF BRANDS

Whilst there are some industry standards and regulations, it is the responsibility of the brand as to how thoroughly they are applied and to what extent they audit their factories. Some companies, such as Nike, H&M and Puma, oversee in great depth and detail how their manufacturers manage themselves and their employees, and act quickly against those who default on agreements. Their standards and procedures are stated clearly on their company websites, whereas other organisations in the industry maintain the bare minimum of regulations, and some companies ignore them completely.

THE FAIR LABOR ASSOCIATION

The F.L.A. was set up at the end of the 90s by a collaboration of socially responsible companies, universities and civil organisations to improve factories around the world by setting up a workplace code of conduct based on ILO (International Labor Organisation) standards, creating systems and processes to help achieve these standards. Many of the big players, such as Nike, P.V.H. and H&M, are affiliate companies as are many others as well.

INTERCONNECTED FOR THE FUTURE

It is important to remember that all the above approaches are connected. Corporate responsibility, compliance and sustainability are all interconnected, with supply chain management as a by-product, and whilst there have been strong moves from the corporate companies to extend best practice by the adoption of agreed standards, there are still plenty of organisations who haven't done so. The developers of today have a chance to help in securing the future of this business. The universal adoption of the above ideals would be a small, but significant step towards a greater goal.

INSIDER PERSPECTIVE
Damien Donnelly

Damien Donnelly is the Senior Fit Manager at Calvin Klein Europe BV. He graduated with a degree in fashion and textiles from The Grafton Academy in Dublin, Ireland and was selected by Irish Tatler Magazine as one of Irelands top graduating designers. After starting in the industry designing small collections of clothing and handbags, Damien turned his attention to pattern making.

His previous work experience has been as both freelance and full time pattern maker for various brands and ateliers in Paris and London, including Reisse and Coast. In 2006 Damien relocated to Amsterdam and worked first at Pepe Jeans and then in 2010 for G-Star. Damien is still based in Amsterdam.

187

What are your top 3 tips for developing a fashion collection from the perspective of your profession?

1) Forecast of fits - if new fits/shapes are pre-selected for your collection, based on fashion forecasts, the pattern team can begin working on the new shapes while the design team finalizes design details. Perfecting the fit will take longer than adding collar shapes and style lines and, if done ahead of time, the designers can receive an actual toile of the new fit to cut, draw and design on.

2) Clarity of design - fashion drawing comes with a wide range of handwriting styles, from simple flat sketches to fully illustrated designs, but remember, at the end of the day, the pattern and production teams need to be able to clearly read these sketches and gather all constructional information from them; can you see exactly where the seams come from - do they have a purpose, it is a pleat or a dart, are there concealed zips, hidden snaps and rivets, what about the finishing on the inside - linings, bound seams, French seams. A technical pack will be delivered to the factory in the end, but this is also invaluable to the pattern makers at the beginning. A beautiful sketch will not produce a beautiful garment unless everyone involved is clear with regard to what is being asked of them.

3) Continuity of communication - the design process, from initial sketch to finalized flat drawing - which your producing factory will receive and work from - is a journey of updates and changes. It is imperative, in order to eliminate last minute problems in the production stages when time is scarce and expensive, that your design, pattern and production teams are aware of all changes. I am frequently amazed when sketches are updated in the final hour and sent only to factories, without pattern makers being

informed, resulting in factories receiving sketches which do not match patterns and often the factory, with little time to produce sales samples, will randomly pick one or the other to work from or alter one to match the other.

What, in your opinion is the most misconceived idea of the fashion industry?

The universal opinion seems still to be that the fashion industry is a fun, flirty and frivolous 24/7 party and yet anyone who works within the industry can testify to 15 hours work days, unending and ever shortening deadlines, last minute changes to entire collections, far off factory visits to the middle of nowhere, where your day starts with a 2 hour drive to the factory at 6.30am and ends at 11.30pm when you finally return to the hotel, having been entertained by the factory heads leaving you with just enough time to take a shower and attend to your work emails. It is true that there are parties - usually when collections are finished and most of the teams are too tired to lift the glass of wine let alone cheer to the fact that finally you have two days of down time before the next season is weighing down on your back once again.

What are the 3 things a developer/ production coordinator should understand from the perspective of your role?

1) I think it is vital that every designer knows the correct balance between a good pattern and a good fabric selection. Both elements, when perfected, will produce a winning finished garment, but if the pattern maker produces a wonderful tailored jacket pattern to accompany a lightweight wool and the designer decides he also wants a

leather jacket version - the result will be something for the bin if the same pattern is used for both. Pattern making, while mathematical, is also about drape, touch and feel, respecting the construction of the fabric and constructing a pattern that compliments this.

2) Designers and pattern makers are creators and this is a time consuming process, but usually time is the one thing that is limited. An understanding on both sides needs to be created and firmly understood. Carried over styles from previous seasons with little touch-ups will not take up much time for the pattern maker, but the development of new shapes is a whole other story. This is where a well-planned 'forecast of fits' becomes essential to working within the time constraints. Often the designer cannot express what he truly needs until he can see a sewn-up shape, and yet the pattern maker must understand what is being asked of him before he can create this sewn-up shape. This is a battle against time, and yet the more time you can devote to this, the less work you will need to do later on.

3) A good pattern maker should be a good craftsman, and the patterns he produces should be respected. Designers and production teams need to have a basic awareness of what happens if they change measurements later on in the development process, especially, if pattern departments cannot be consulted. If the shoulder looks too small and you increase the width, be aware that you will also have to change other measurements that are affected by this. The smallest change can affect so many other parts in terms of measurements.

INSIDER PERSPECTIVE
Pauline Cheung

(www.peonyrice.com)
(www.industria-collective.com)

Pauline Cheung is the director of Industria Collective Ltd and founder / CD for Peony Rice, a womenswear and accessory label based in Hong Kong and Shanghai. With her area of expertise being predominantly womenswear, Pauline gained extensive experience internationally as design director at DKNY, and later, as head of operations and product development at Ports 1961.

After relocating back to Hong Kong in 2006, Pauline switched her focus to eco sourcing, brand building and developing links with sustainable communities in South East Asia, and started Peony Rice, an ethical fashion and lifestyle brand that is sourced and produced responsibly in Asia through collaborations with local communities. Pauline is based in Hong Kong and Shanghai.

**What are your top 3 tips for developing
a fashion collection from the perspective
of your profession?**

1) Consider the environment and future
generations and the garments that you are
producing.

2) Consider your customers - understand
them - emotions, lifestyle, environment,
practicality, and give them want they want
and something a little more. It is fashion.

3) Create a desirable product and have fun
with it. Fashion is serious, but not to be taken
SO seriously. It should make a person happy...

**What, in your opinion is the most
misconceived idea of the fashion
industry?**

That it is all glam, parties and celebs.
Although the fashion industry is a very
powerful one and it can have a lot of
influence over daily lives, it requires a lot of
hard work and discipline also.

**What are the 3 things a developer/
production coordinator should
understand from the perspective of your
role?**

The target customer and how they are going
to look in the clothes - reality check. Being
in tune with the market needs thorough
research and street level focus. One focused
story for all.

INSIDER
PERSPECTIVE
Nicolas Steele

(www.nicolassteele.com/collection)

Nicolas Steele is the founder of the brand NICOLAS STEELE, a menswear label based in Italy. After completing art school in England, the early part of his career included working with Katherine Hamnett and John Richmond. In 1998 Nicolas began working with Gucci under the direction of Tom Ford, and for eight years served as a design director, collaborating with all the departments of the brand. In 2000 he extended his responsibilities to working with Yves Saint Laurent.

In 2006 he left the Gucci group in order to start his own consulting company, working with a varied roster of clients, among them Calvin Klein, Tom Ford, Oscar de la Renta, Valentino, Balmain and Tommy Hilfiger. In 2009 the brand NICOLAS STEELE was launched to address his own personal need for an artisanal product that focuses on a contemporary client. Nicolas is based in Italy.

What are your top 3 tips for developing a fashion collection from the perspective of your profession?

1) Have a factory, may be an obvious one, but it is the most important. Also, be economically aware of all the costs involved overall before you embark on a relationship with a factory. Be careful with your working relationships with the factories. Always maintain honest, respectful and clear relationships with them, as the industry is small and people remember.

2) An interest in fashion on a practical level is important, and be aware of your own personal taste level. Be aware of trends in fashion, don't be a slave to them, but be informed so you recognise the cultural and style references when they are mentioned.

3) Have a sense of humor; don't take it too seriously, keep a distance and keep things in perspective. This is a business run on emotion.

What, in your opinion is the most misconceived idea of the fashion industry?

That it is fun and that the people are nice. It is a business like anything else, and it is no longer as easy going as it used to be. The luxury market used to be more aspirationally driven and less corporate. Everything now is more corporate and more management than design driven. This is not to say it is a bad thing, but it is not always good either, and will ultimately impact the consumer in the end if taken to extremes. It is about value for both the brand & the customer on all levels.

What are the 3 things a developer/ production coordinator should understand from the perspective of your role?

1) The best production people tend to be those who studied design (although not a rule), who have knowledge of how things are constructed and how a pattern is made. They may have realised that designing wasn't their true calling and decided to follow the technical side instead. This group tends to understand the role of production on a level more in tune with designer. They combine a level of finishing with the practical understanding of the process.

2) You need to be able to communicate with the designer in an open manner so as to understand what they want, what their vision is. A good designer will be open to practicalities and will respond to alternative options, but it should always be their vision. An inexperienced designer may not be quite so open minded, so it is best to have a plan B prepared for when their idea isn't technically possible. Always be prepared to be flexible with the designer and also with the factory. Be clear about the passing on of information, don't leave any room for misunderstandings, and if you are not sure, ask the designer or factory to be clear, even if it means asking 3 times.

3) As a developer you don't need to know about the business aspects, like marketing, and sales, but as you get more experienced it will add to your skill set and give you more awareness of the bigger picture.

INSIDER PERSPECTIVE
Melanie Tebbutt

Melanie Tebbutt is Head of product development RTW at Hunter Boot Ltd. After setting up and running her own street-wear brand in London for 3 years, Melanie worked on the technical side of the industry in areas of pattern cutting, sampling and production for small UK based brands. In 2004 she graduated from the London College of Fashion in the field of Product Development, and moved to Amsterdam taking up a position in product development within the Sport Performance division at Nike.

In 2010 Melanie moved to Tommy Hilfiger Europe, working exclusively on the runway collection in the role of product manager, then the UK to take up a position at Burberry. In 2012 she moved to Calvin Klein Europe. She is now based in London.

What are your top 3 tips for developing a fashion collection from the perspective of your profession?

1) Be prepared to be extremely flexible, ready to adapt to change and to think on your feet. Push boundaries with ideas of others and your own. Trouble shooting is a big part of the role.

2) As a developer you are in the middle between the creative, the technical and the business people. Respect and understand everyone's deadlines and agendas.

3) Build strong relationships with external vendors with mutual respect. All new relationships take some time to build. The more you put into them initially will help the product to develop. Ensure you understand their values from the outset, which will help the respect factor from both sides. Give clear expectations, share your goals and monitor performance.

What, in your opinion is the most misconceived idea of the fashion industry?

The glamour. Traveling to different countries sounds fun. It can be, but be prepared to spend most of your time on the road, in factories in jetlagged mode. During a two week preparation on set for New York Fashion Week, I worked solidly for 14 days, with just one day off. Running around for samples and making calls around the clock to all time zones. At one point I was in the back of a FedEx van hunting for missing boxes. Not so glamorous!

What are the 3 things a developer/ production coordinator should understand from the perspective of your role?

1) Ensure all raw materials are sourced from the same country of origin as the garment of manufacture, or within countries which benefit positively from duties. Especially if GP targets and lead time are part of the range plan strategy.

2) Be extremely conscious of lead times for both raw material and garment production. Calendar discipline is a must for approving of raw materials and garment fit to meet delivery dates and price negotiation.

3) If developing a commercial collection, always keep the target FOB-s in mind when pre-selecting fabrics for design. Calculate a pre-cost before signing off designs for sampling. Have a plan B if exceeding targets to present at proto review. If the style is a revenue driver, it will help to balance the weighted margin. Be conscious of fabric minimums within the range plan for production planning.

INSIDER PERSPECTIVE
Constantino Ferrandino

Costantino Ferrandino is the export manager for the Italian fabric manufacturer Cotonificio Veneto SPA. After graduating from University Ca'Foscari di Venezia in 1992 with a degree in Economics, Costa started as export manager for Montebello SPA and remained there for 3 years before moving to Cotonificio Veneto SPA in 1998 as divisional manager.

Following additional moves within the textile industry to Textile Solution, Textile Italu and GTE Trebor, Constantino returned to Cotonificio Veneto in 2003, where he remains to this day with his focus being on the management of the international sales team and independent agents. Costantino is based in Italy.

What are your top 3 tips for developing a fashion collection from the perspective of your profession?

1) Deep knowledge of lifestyle trends; it is useless to develop fabrics for garments that are against the trends that the whole population follows. You must develop materials people like to wear.

2) Deep knowledge of your company; you must make products you can produce in time and at a "good enough" price. Only when you know very well the "car you are driving" you can do that.

3) To listen very carefully to your target customers and trend setter for a fine tuning of your collection season by season.

What, in your opinion is the most misconceived idea of the fashion industry?

To me it's the idea that fashion is frivolous, evanescent, impalpable. Fashion is an industry, it is a business; as concrete and substantial as all other businesses.

What are the 3 things a developer/ production coordinator should understand from the perspective of your role?

1) That to have a technical knowledge, even basic, helps a lot.

2) That this business is the art of balancing all factors above. When one of those is too dominant, then in the long term the company suffers; today there are many marketing oriented companies and they are also successful, but many of them they are exploiting the value of their brand, a value often accumulated through many years of design investments; those "marketing driven" managers will leave the company sooner or later and the value of the company and its brand will not be the same any more. On the other side, a company just "design driven" will suffer in terms of growth, ability to attract resources (human, financial, …) and most of the time will remain beautiful and small.

3) That fabric producers are not like a supermarket. To develop long term relationships pays, in terms of money and stress. I could mention many examples from all over Europe. And … let me add, it pays back also in term of less wasted paper: when I am called to sign hundreds of pages of contracts that try to rule every single aspect of the business relationship between a fabric supplier and a customer I really think they are wasted trees and money.

197

INSIDER PERSPECTIVE
Sandra de Gooyer

Sandra de Gooyer is Senior Product Developer for Karl Lagerfeld, an international brand based in The Netherlands.

After graduating from the Hogeschool Enschede in 1998, Sandra has worked as a production developer, buying manager, fabric buyer and product coordinator for companies, such as Mexx, Oilily and Vanilia. With varied work experience in the development, quality and production areas, Sandra is now focusing on her passion of fabric sourcing, from initial selection to bulk delivery. Sandra is based in Amsterdam.

What are your top 3 tips for developing a fashion collection from the perspective of your profession?

1) Stay true to your DNA when designing a collection, it is okay to follow on trends, but start from your own/company strength.

2) Make sure everybody works according the line plan and is aware of the price points, so you will not get in trouble with prices when you are already too far into the process. What often happens is that a fabric needs to be replaced from sampling to bulk. Nine out of ten times the style will get dropped at a later stage because no good replacement can be found, after hours of extra work = lots of money in fabric research and already selling the style by your sales team. Plus disappointed customers who do not get the expected product.

3) Dare to take a decision; it will make your collection only stronger (following no. 2).

What, in your opinion is the most misconceived idea of the fashion industry?

That it is all about hip and happening.

What are the 3 things a developer/ production coordinator should understand from the perspective of your role?

From my perspective as a fabric buyer/ technician, it is important that a developer knows some basics about certain fabrics and how you can solve these with workmanship of the product. Like silk, linen and voile for example. And knowledge on pricing, so that when a designer picks an expensive fabric the styling needs to be simple.

INSIDER PERSPECTIVE
Jonathan Hansen

Jonathan Hansen works as a director of design and product development in the home goods and fashion industries. Jonathan has worked in the product design and development industries for the past 15 years. He was the director of global production and sourcing at Thom Browne during its explosive growth starting in 2007.

With a background in home product design, product development and supply chain management, Jonathan has used his experience and extensive contacts to become an independent consultant in design and product development. He is based New York.

What are your top 3 tips for developing a fashion collection from the perspective of your profession?

1) Designing the "back end" of the company is just as important as designing the front end product. It is easy to get hyper-focused on the product one is selling. All the details: fit, fabric, trim and brand aesthetic, consume endless amounts of time. It is important to put the same level of attention and effort towards the back end. Developing an effective product development system, efficient and financially conscious production management, and a sound sales inventory and fulfillment system are essential to building a well thought out fashion brand. In short, making sure there is the equal attention put to both sides. In general, it is usually the business side that suffers when it comes to starting a fashion brand. Being conscious about formulating the back end system with the same level of detail is essential to being successful.

2) Design, sales & production must communicate seamlessly. It is a team effort to ensure that the right product is made, produced and sold.

3) Know who you are and stick with it. Having a clear aesthetic, combined with a clear business framework, is essential. Know who you are means that if you are a street wear brand your business approach will be different than if you are in fashion accessories or a luxury clothing brand. Every business has a different way of taking their aesthetic and connecting it with a business framework, marketing and sales strategy. The product and the business plan should be aligned to who you are.

What, in your opinion is the most misconceived idea of the fashion industry?

It is that a fashion brand is all about the product. My experience is that many times, on the face of it, the appearance is all about the glossy product that's sold in the press. If you want to be successful you need to understand that there are two words, fashion and business. It has to be grounded in the reality that what you are building is actually a business and is there to make money, and not just to be a vanity product.

What are the 3 things a developer/production coordinator should understand from the perspective of your role?

1) Spend money on the things that make money, not on the things that don't. Things that don't make money: fancy business cards and stationary, fancy office furniture, expensive business meals, pointless office supplies, perks that are not in line with the financial reality of the company.

2) Build a complete brand that offers the same look, feel and service across all dimensions of the business. There are many ways that people touch the brand, whether it is the end consumer, a vendor, a wholesale buyer, or someone in the press. Creating a unified brand voice will help build the brand in a more focused manner. These impact on the way people perceive a brand by unifying the brand identity across all the channels in which it has contact with people.

3) Develop a system for communicating between design, sales & production that ensures complete transfer of product info, known material minimums, factory minimums, time lines, etc.

INSIDER PERSPECTIVE
Michael Arts

Michael Arts is on the management of PVH Corp. With his area of expertise of sales, merchandising, product development and brand building, Michael started out in the mid 1980's at Scapa of Scotland, later moving to Bellerose Europe in 1988.

Following 6 years at Polo Ralph Lauren Europe, Michael joined the management team at Tommy Hilfiger Europe where he remained until early 2011. He is based in Amsterdam.

What are your top 3 tips for developing a fashion collection from the perspective of your profession?

1) Stay nervous; anyone who is over confident is bound to fail.

2) You need to have taste. You need to have an educated taste. People talk about taste level and viewpoint about bad taste versus good taste, and ultimately, you need to have a good taste level and it needs to be consistent and whole.

3) You have to have someone to control you when developing a range. You need to have someone that you respect enough to allow them to control you. In general, lifestyle brands spend too much time on the tip of the pyramid rather than the base (the 'all year round' money). It is like a reverse pyramid when it comes to the range plan. The range plan pyramid is in place, but rather than spending the bulk of development time on the base, which makes the money all year round, the creative merchandise companies spend all the time on the tip, the top level, and that's where it goes wrong. It should be about spending energy on the base of the pyramid as much as on the top of the pyramid, everything in between will be a derivative of energy spend on base and top.

4) Anyone who says 'know your customer' is lying. Customers today are very unpredictable and equally hard to second guess.

5) There is too much 'last year-itis' in companies where the bulk of the range is formulated from previous styles, which are re-coloured or re-fabricated. There should be empathy towards it, but it must have its place. It should be about creating newness to a collection

What, in your opinion is the most misconceived idea of the fashion industry?

That it's glamorous. The industry is hard work!

What are the 3 things a developer/ production coordinator should understand from the perspective of your role?

1) That there is an understandable message which people can work towards. Too many people work with their own opinions.

2) You need to have a statement, a merchandisable statement, that a consumer can understand. It starts at the beginning of a season as 100% and by the end of the process when the product comes out it has been filtered out to around 20% of the original idea and this is confusing to the customer. It is a misnomer that companies 'own an idea'; no one owns anything, you constantly need to re-emphasize who you are.

3) Show love for the product. It must be an emotional process.

INSIDER PERSPECTIVE
Johannes Egler

Professor Johannes W. Egler is a lecturer in Fashion Design, Collection Design, Fashion Production, and Merchandising at both F.I.T. in New York and Polimoda in Florence, Italy.

After graduating in Artistic and Industrial textile design at the Kunstakademie of Linz in Austria, he specialized in fashion design and has contributed to many labels, including his current involvement as senior designer at the International label, ROSSO 35, in Italy. His Active Sportswear collection was produced and distributed by Reebok U.S.A. in 1992. Johannes is based in Italy.

What are your top 3 tips for developing a fashion collection from the perspective of your profession?

1) Reflect well on your color choices; color in fashion is so important.

2) Define the silhouette.

3) Select interesting new materials and fabrics.

What, in your opinion is the most misconceived idea of the fashion industry?

The most misconceived idea, in my opinion, is thinking that to copy is a key to success.

What are the 3 things a developer/ production coordinator should understand from the perspective of your role?

1) To understand who you are designing for; there is a lot of misinterpretation of target; to understand what use, function and meaning the product has for your customer.

2) How to invest in an independent design concept and how to develop it.

3) Product development is team work; so, to understand how to create an operating team that considers design, marketing strategy and production as active interaction.

INSIDER
PERSPECTIVE
Ehud Joseph

Ehud Joseph is a menswear designer. An Israeli-born New Zealander, Ehud trained originally as an artist and graduated with a degree in printmaking. After that he studied pattern making at Massey University in Wellington before setting up his own company and moving to London, where he completed an MA in menswear at Central St Martins.

Ehud has worked for high street and luxury brands, and has had his own menswear label, Ehud, which specializes in clean lines and fine tailoring. His industry achievements include showing his line in the official Paris Fashion Week schedule. Ehud is based in Amsterdam.

What are your top 3 tips for developing a fashion collection from the perspective of your profession?

1) Know who you are as a designer. It is too easy to get carried away with fantasy and to compare yourself with other companies and other designers. For longevity, the trick is to know who you are and focus on that as the primary aspect of the brand identity and the core of the collection.

2) Know your customer, and that means be clear about who you want to dress and that is to say the market. It is easy to say you are designing for 25-35 year olds that buy *Vogue*, but I think you need to be more specific and really go into the shops, see what products they buy, how much they spend and what products the stores actually sell. Compare this to who you are. Angle your collection to suit that, but this should always come after the aspect of knowing who you are as a designer.

3) Know how you are going to build your name, the strategy behind it. It is really a financial thing; be clear of your product, your price range and your customer. Where do the shops buy their product? Which trade shows do they attend? Do they go to the fashion shows? Probably not! Do they work with specific sales agencies? Look into this and then construct the way that you are going to make and price your clothes and sell them. You should try to make it understandable for the buyers. It is not a creative process but it is the reality.

What, in your opinion is the most misconceived idea of the fashion industry?

That creativity sells. It doesn't, not now, maybe 10 years ago, but I think that the market now is targeted at selling. I think that what people buy, especially in the luxury sector, are well-designed garments, which are easy to understand. Most collections that we look at on the catwalk from the designers that we admire, those aren't even the collections that are in-store as they sell the pre collections and cruise collection for 8 months of the year. It is a fantasy, and I think the difference between press pieces and show pieces and real pieces is so big that you really need to understand there is a huge difference.

What are the 3 things a developer/ production coordinator should understand from the perspective of your role?

1) What is the customer expecting in terms of quality for the price?

2) What the shape of the body of the customer is. For instance, getting a 16 year old twig to do your fittings even when you turn that proportionally up so the waist is the same size, but nobody can fit their arse into it, is a problem. Be aware of where you are selling and what the body shape is for the market.

3) It is also very important to know that you can draw a sketch and make a garment, but that is not where it ends. Garments need to be developed and the development takes time. So, you need to prioritise your timetable in such a way that there is enough time to develop a garment fully. It is so obvious when garments aren't developed fully, because that's when you see the poor proportions and that's when things don't work. It is important to recognize this, so it is quite common to be designing much earlier in the season than you would normally expect to in order to have enough time to let the garments mature. It easy to make something look good on paper, whereas in reality it doesn't work.

INSIDER PERSPECTIVE
Fiona Jenvey

(www.mpdclick.com)

Fiona Jenvey is the CEO of Mudpie, a trend forecasting company, which offers an online service, trend books and consultancy. After graduating from The London College of Fashion and working within the industry as a commercial designer, Fiona founded Mudpie in 1992 and has used her ability to combine commercial design and future trends to make Mudpie a front runner in the trend forecasting industry, covering the adult, youth and children's markets.

Fiona is an accomplished industry speaker, and has been sponsored to give seminars internationally on trend intelligence, and advises brands, retailers, and international trade organisations on innovation, trends, consumer insight and design. Fiona is based on the South Coast of the UK.

What are your top 3 tips for developing a fashion collection from the perspective of your profession?

I would always suggest differentiating the product. Many brands reference the runway. I would suggest first understanding the feelings of the consumer and then develop a collection around that. Get the emotional elements right; these are generally colour, shape and the tactile elements or materials.

What, in your opinion is the most misconceived idea of the fashion industry?

The volume fashion retailer has done nothing for the fashion industry. Fashion is a form of design art. The cheap product we see today is simply 'clothing'. Real fashion does not need to be expensive, but should be considered a 'created' product. A student who customises a few reused pieces has created fashion, and this is not expensive.

What are the 3 things a developer/ production coordinator should understand from the perspective of your role?

1) Consumer trends are the most important; by this I mean lifestyle trends, spending habits, social attitudes etc. This is the most involved aspect of trend research, and the most specialist.

2) Understanding the trend, for example, for the Autmn/Winter 12/13 season we forecast a trend called Myriad. This is based around the Middle East and was forecast and published before the Arab Spring uprisings. The trend is based around three elements, Luxury, Sustainability and a focus on the Arab world. Designers often think that because we are talking Arabia we need to feature a camel on the artwork, but miss the point of sustainability and the New City of Masdar, probably the world's most important live experiment on sustainable living (Abu Dhabi).

3) The duration of a trend. Clearly, Kate Middleton's engagement dress, a particular runway style or a look on the red carpet all make great quick fix fashion trends and represent a snapshot in time. These are trends to get on the shop floor within a few weeks. The trend for sustainability has only just started and will be a 20 year trend and will involve the inclusion of man-made and natural fibres new to the fashion industry. Use of water, chemicals, sources of power and labour practices will all form part of this evolving process.

INSIDER
PERSPECTIVE
Peter Som

(www.petersom.com)

Womenswear designer Peter Som specializes in quirky, feminine, yet classic designs worn by Hollywood's elite. Peter graduated Cum Laude in Art History from Connecticut College in 1993 and continued his studies at Parsons School of Design, where he was a recipient of the Isaac Mizrahi Gold Thimble Award. While at Parsons, he apprenticed with two of America's most revered designers – Michael Kors and Calvin Klein.

In 2001, Peter made his mark on the fashion world with his debut collection at Bryant Park. From 2007 to 2008 he served as creative director of women's wear for the legendary Bill Blass. He was nominated twice for the CFDA Perry Ellis Award for Emerging Talent and was a finalist for the Cooper Hewitt National Design Award for Fashion Design.

What are your top 3 tips for developing a fashion collection from the perspective of your profession?

1) Have a point of view – what sets you apart from the rest of the field, which is so crowded, is how you stand out and what makes you different. That is the most important thing. Customers can sense authenticity or can sense if you are not true to yourself, which is the core aspect. Have a vision and know what you are about.

2) Take advice. Fashion is a business, it is not only the creative side, so much is the actual business, otherwise it would be a hobby. Take advice from the sales side of the business and from the merchandising side. It is important to maintain a balance. In the first point you have a vision, but in the second point you need to have an open mind. Listen to what the stores say, as these are people with experience and know about what's going to sell and how certain things work.

3) It is not just about designing a pretty dress; there are so many steps along that line once the dress is even made until it sits on the shop floor. Be a sponge and take in all the information. For a lot of designers, I think the ego can get in the way, and the fact is the industry is so much work and so many small steps to that end product that's sitting in the stores and it is not so obvious or so direct a line so it is important to speak to everyone.

4) Get a business partner if you are the creative person. This is about running a business and there's only so much one person can do. If you look at any successful designer in the history of fashion, they had a successful business partner beside them. Look at Tom Ford, Yves Saint Laurent or Valentino. If there is someone next to you, it will improve your chances of success. It is a rare occasion when a designer can handle every single aspect of running a company, so when you start out and if you can't have someone full time, try to have someone like a consultant or adviser in the industry who can be someone you can talk to.

What, in your opinion is the most misconceived idea of the fashion industry?

It is a glamour industry – the models, the fashion show, it is so much work and I think as a designer your quote unquote moment of glamour is right when you take a bow and it lasts for a nanosecond. You really have to love it like there's no tomorrow, as it really is so much work – just on the design side. For the perceived glamour – that's the irony, there is a lot of smoke and mirrors that has to happen. At the end of the day, yes, with the clothing line, you are selling a dream, a fantasy and a lifestyle, but it takes a lot of work to make it effortless, so if you are going in expecting something instantaneous or that everything you are going to do is going to be fabulous, think again and think long and hard. You'll be working night and day when you start, so if it all feels like work, you are going to have a short career.

**What are the 3 things a developer/
production coordinator should
understand from the perspective of your
role?**

1) It is a 2-way street; you need to know
what information to give the developer in
order for them to work well. Sometimes one
of the most important things from my side
as a designer is to know what information
to give to them, so that they can carry out
the sketch development or source the fabric,
because the focus comes from the top. For
someone in the design staff, a lot of it is
about creative problem solving; finding
options of fabrics when the one I wanted is
not available. To go a step further and show
what the options are. With my team in New
York, there is shorthand and that does come
with time. When you are working with a
creative person, sometimes it is not super
easy, sometimes the creative person can't
fully articulate what they are thinking about,
so they are also looking to you, the developer
to bring something to the table.

2) It is all about collaboration and creative
dialogue and it is important to bring
something to the table, but also, not just
any random idea, they have to make sense
for the brand. Have an open mind – it is
collaboration and a balancing act.

THE KEY DATES
calendar

Most companies I know of have a key dates calendar. Under a variety of names (dates and gates, design calendar or year plan) the key dates calendar is a set of important deadlines from the start of development to the end of production of a collection. A key dates calendar drives the development and production process and enables all individuals involved to plan, create and produce a range. Every person in the team is aware of the plan and all are encouraged to work according to it.

I would recommend anyone in the business of planning a range to take the time and set up a template for a key dates calendar and save it, so it can be amended season after season for ease and speed. There is logic to the setup of the calendar, and once created, it can be transferred from season to season with minimal alteration.

As with any planning, it should begin with the end point and working backwards to find the starting point. In this case, we start with the bulk shipment of production, and work back to designer research. The 10 key stages at the top of the calendar are the most important. The rest can be flexible around these dates. Remember that it is always better to plan more steps into the chart then fewer; easier to remove some and have more time available than having to add in steps.

I must stress that none of the timings in the fold out calendar are set in stone. They are approximations, as every brand, designer and company works to different schedules. They will, however, give you an idea and a guideline.

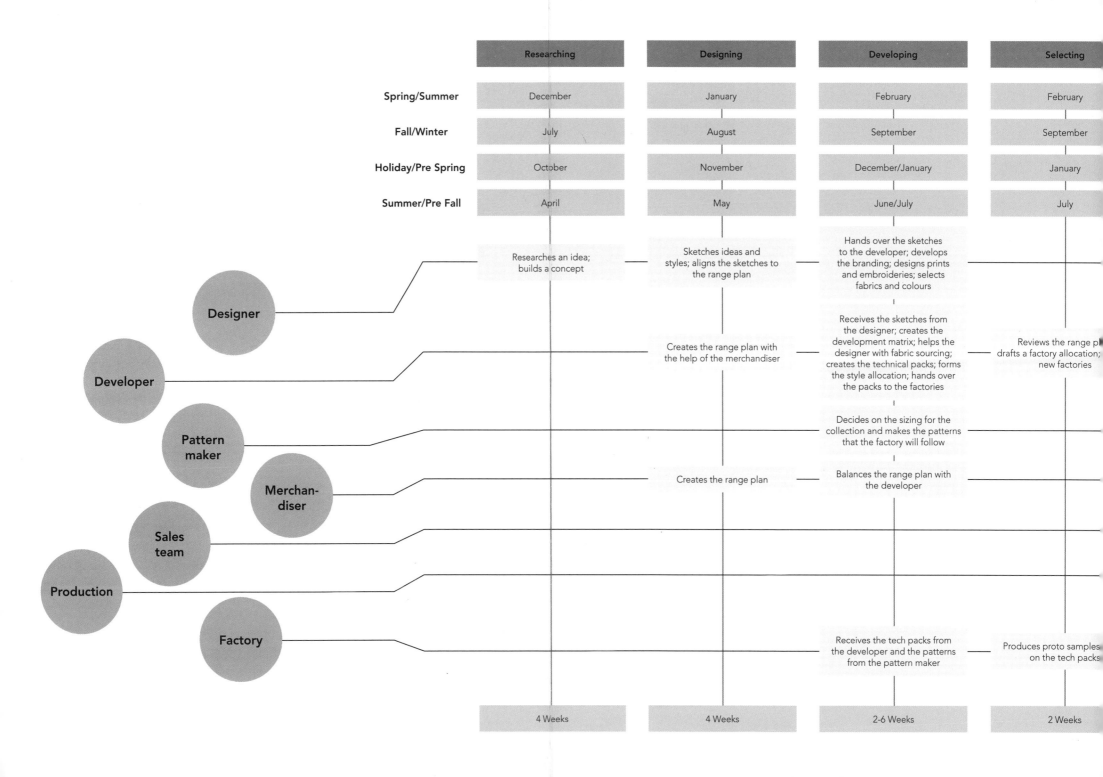

	Researching	Designing	Developing	Selecting
Spring/Summer	December	January	February	February
Fall/Winter	July	August	September	September
Holiday/Pre Spring	October	November	December/January	January
Summer/Pre Fall	April	May	June/July	July

Designer — Researches an idea; builds a concept — Sketches ideas and styles; aligns the sketches to the range plan — Hands over the sketches to the developer; develops the branding; designs prints and embroideries; selects fabrics and colours

Developer — Creates the range plan with the help of the merchandiser — Receives the sketches from the designer; creates the development matrix; helps the designer with fabric sourcing; creates the technical packs; forms the style allocation; hands over the packs to the factories — Reviews the range p▮ drafts a factory allocation; new factories

Pattern maker — Decides on the sizing for the collection and makes the patterns that the factory will follow

Merchandiser — Creates the range plan — Balances the range plan with the developer

Sales team

Production

Factory — Receives the tech packs from the developer and the patterns from the pattern maker — Produces proto samples on the tech packs

| | 4 Weeks | 4 Weeks | 2-6 Weeks | 2 Weeks |

Reviewing	Preparing	Launching	Analysing	Planning	Producing
April	June	July	July/August	August/September	September/November
October/November	December	January	January/February	February/March	March/June
February	March	April	April/May	May/June	June/September
September	October	November	November	December	January/March
Reviews the prototype samples; makes changes and adjustments; applies the branding	Makes the line book	Visually merchandises the range; launches to the sales teams		Reviews the comments from the sales teams	
Prepares the protos for review; aligns the pricing; makes changes and adjustments; applies the branding; documents the changes; hands over to factory	Finalises the development matrix; receives the final prices from the factories	Receives the samples; fits the key styles; launches to the sales teams			
Assists with the fitting				Works with the production team on fits for production	
Totals the range plan	Creates the line list for selling	Finalises the selling tools; launches to the sales teams	Receives forecasts from the sales team; compiles the sales requests; creates the purchase orders	Finalises the sales figures; sends the purchase orders to the factories	
		Sees the range for the first time	Sells the range		
		Receives production lead times from factories; finalises the prices from the factories		Refits all production styles; creates the production planning; defines the PP sample status; updates all the tech packs; hands over to the factories	Follows the production planning by process, travels to source for QC check
Receives and acts on the developer's comments	Finalises all the cost prices for the developer; sends the finished samples to the warehouse of the brand		Gives production lead times to production team; gives final prices to the production and merchandising teams	Orders the bulk fabric; receives updated tech packs from the production team	Receives the purchase order from the brand; tests the bulk fabric; follows the production process; produces labels, packs and ships the garments
2-4 Weeks	4 Weeks	2 Weeks	4 Weeks	4 Weeks	1-4 Months

THE KEY DATES
calendar

HOLIDAY
closures

Every country in the world has public and religious holidays that are observed by individuals and businesses, and the brands that work with them have to take these into account when planning development and production schedules. As many of these holidays are movable, it is a good idea to establish what holiday observances are likely to affect work schedules and to get the relevant dates every year at the start of the season. Here are a few key holidays that you may encounter in your company.

> CHINESE NEW YEAR
January / February

C.N.Y. is an all East- and South-East-Asia celebration that falls in January-February of each year. The festival begins on the first day of the first month in the traditional Chinese calendar and ends with Lantern festival; it is considered a major holiday for the Chinese and has had influence on the new year celebrations of its geographic neighbors, as well as cultures with whom the Chinese have had extensive interaction. It is not uncommon for manufacturers to close for three weeks in this period, as their workers travel back to their homes to spend time with their families.

Chinese New Year is celebrated in countries and territories with significant Chinese populations, such as Mainland China, Hong Kong, Indonesia, Macau, Malaysia, the Philippines, Singapore, Taiwan and Thailand.

> RAMADAN

Ramadan is a religious period in the ninth month of the Islamic calendar, which lasts 29 or 30 days. For the past two years it has fallen in August–September, but it moves on every year by 11 days, so over a period of some 30 years it occurs in every part of the Gregorian (western) calendar. It is the Islamic month of fasting, during which participating Muslims refrain from eating, drinking and smoking during daylight hours.

Countries that observe Ramadan are Syria, Turkey, Lebanon, Egypt, Malaysia, Iran and all the other Arabic and Islamic countries.

This holiday could affect any sample making or production activity according to when Ramadan occurs in any particular year. For any production planned for an Islamic country, it is a good idea to establish as early as possible the dates of Ramadan in that year and plan accordingly.

> SUMMER HOLIDAY CLOSURE
July / August

Some countries in southern Europe (France, Italy, Spain and Portugal) close for between two and four weeks in July and August. In some cases it is to tie in with the local holidays, but in others because it is simply too hot to work in manufacturing units, so they close.

> DIWALI
October / November / December

Diwali, known as the "festival of lights", takes place between mid-October and mid-December and is celebrated for five days according to the Hindu calendar. It begins in September-October and ends in November-December.

Diwali is an official holiday in many countries around the world; some key locations where production could be placed and therefore be affected would be: India, Sri Lanka, Mauritius, Guyana, Suriname, Malaysia and Singapore.

GLOSSARY
& Index

The process of developing and producing a fashion collection is an exhilarating, creative and repetitive process, filled with specialist terminology and descriptions at every twist and turn. Whether you are forming your own company or starting in an established fashion organisation, you will soon discover that the terminology used is both highly specific and varied.

But the question is, who tells you these terms and how are you supposed to remember them? If you are lucky, you will land yourself in a position in a company that celebrates abbreviations with files listing them, but in others, it is a simple case of writing them in a notebook and referring back when the need occurs.

It can be daunting at first to be that fish out of water, but after a few weeks words and phrases will become familiar as they are thrown around the office like fabric in a sample room. The skill lies in understanding their importance and their relevance in the procedures you are enacting, so here, in the glossary, are the key terms and general rules and tools explained for your reference.

AGENT
An agent for manufacturing is usually a one-person operation whose aim is to introduce the factory to the brand and provide a basic level of interaction between the two parties. › pp. 52, 67, 115, 143, 183

ATELIER
An atelier is a small to medium sized workshop set up for high end luxury products. The atelier studio works with an artisan approach, meaning, that in most cases the fabric is cut by hand instead of on automated cutting tables and the makers make entire garments rather than just one small part. › pp. 112, 115, 124

BLOCK
A 'block' is a basic pattern, which is made with the specific customer measurements for the brand. › p. 83

BRANDING
Branding is a method of adding the name of the company or brand onto a garment. Buttons, labels and zippers can all carry the company name or logo, and this helps the customer to differentiate between one company and another. › pp. 16, 94, 145, 158

BUY
The buy is another word for the total order quantity that the shops have ordered and which is made by the factory. › pp. 66, 173

BUYING OFFICE
A buying office operates in a similar manner to an agent in providing a link between the brand and the factory, but is a larger organization, comprising account managers who can take sole responsibility for the brand's account. › pp. 114, 136

CALLING OFF TRIMS
Calling off trims is the process whereby the brand or factories contact the trim company to order trims. › p. 97

CATWALK LINE
A catwalk line has between two and four collections of garments a year and shows at one of the many international Fashion Weeks (for example, New York or Milan). The shows contain a mixture of commercial styles that buyers will order for their stores, and press pieces, which magazines will feature in fashion shoots. Catwalk shows are used by many high street brands as an indication for new trend directions. › pp. 113, 164

CIF
This is a method of supplying goods from a manufacturer to a brand, which includes all costs for the garment manufacture in addition to the full cost of transportation to the brand's nominated location (usually the brand's central warehouse). › p. 146

CMT
CMT means Cut / Make / Trim. It literally means that the factory only costs these elements in the price, not the fabric cost. This is bought directly by the brand and not by the factory. › pp. 121, 146

COLLECTION
A collection is the collective name for a group of garments that are linked together by a concept or theme. An alternative word or phrase for collection is range, or range of garments. › pp. 16, 22, 31, 45, 66, 88, 155, 168, 177

COLOUR CARD
A colour card (or colour palette) is a selection of shades compiled by the design or concept team, which gives a colour direction for the season. › pp. 23, 53, 60, 133, 169

COLOUR OFFER

The colour offer is the range of colours in which the style can be bought. › p. 169

CONCEPT

A concept is a design direction for the colour, silhouette, mood and fabric brief for the range. Usually it comprises magazine images showing lifestyle shots, colour examples, fabric pieces (swatches) or even historical books, poems or songs. The concept creates the mood of the collection and is always open to different interpretations. › pp. 15, 18, 22, 44, 52, 60, 79, 95, 112, 132, 143, 150, 165, 176

COST PRICE

The cost price is the cost of making the goods by the factory. It can be given in two different forms: CIF and FOB. The majority of brands prefer to work with FOB costs. › pp. 40, 45, 57, 99, 115, 122, 128, 146, 151

DEVELOPMENT MATRIX

The development matrix is the central place for the keeping of all the information for the whole collection; it can be an Excel chart, which holds the majority of the details of the tech packs for the collection. › pp. 18, 76, 88, 133, 144, 150

FABRIC

Fabric and textiles are names for the material from which clothes are made. › pp. 14, 18, 23, 27, 30, 36, 44, 101, 113, 122, 125, 142, 168, 184

FASHION ILLUSTRATION

A fashion illustration is really a beautiful piece of work and not at all technical in its appearance (it has no measurements).
In some cases the designer will make a 'flat' technical sketch with measurements to sit alongside it, so that the developers or factory can gauge proportion and shape. › p. 172

FIT

A 'fit' is a description to explain the silhouette of a garment and refers to a set of measurements, which can make a garment tight or loose. These measurements are carefully constructed by the pattern maker to ensure that the proportions of the garment are correct and that the fit is appropriate for the end customer. › pp. 24, 39, 82, 126, 136, 150

FLAT TECHNICAL SKETCH

The flat sketch is a structured computer sketch that is used to give an idea of proportion and scale to the style. The sketch has to be a very simple image so that a 'non creative' person can understand what the garment will look like. It needs to be clear in its details of pocket placement, collar shape, button addition etc., as this is what the factory will work from. These sketches are in the correct colours and fabrics for the season and are used much later as a selling aid for the sales teams. › pp. 81, 142, 157

FOB

FOB (Free On Board) is a shipping method for the goods in which the factory pays for the total cost of the goods, the fabric, the cutting, the making and the trims, and partial transport costs (up to the port or location of departure for the goods but not including the full cost of transportation). It is a term that means the factory pays for all of the garment manufacturing. › pp. 146, 152, 159

GREIGE

Greige fabric is un-dyed, unfinished fabric, and is often ordered by brands when they are not yet in a position to select colours. › p. 54

HANDLOOM

A handloom is a small swatch of fabric made up on a handloom by the fabric mill to show a particular design. › p. 61

HANGTAG

A hangtag is an item of branding which hangs on the garment when it is in the stores. It can be made of card or fabric and holds information within a barcode of the style name, the price and the size. › pp. 19, 101, 125, 184

HEADER CARD

A header card is a square of fabric (can be up to 30cm x 30cm) from the fabric mill with its technical details written on the top for reference. This will include the reference code for the fabric, the price, the colour reference number, the weight per m², the width and composition (100% wool, or 70% wool 30% cashmere, etc.). › p. 55

INCOTERMS

Incoterms are an internationally agreed set of terms for the costs associated with the transportation of goods. These costs can vary according to who pays for the various parts of the process of getting the goods from the factory to the brand's warehouse. › pp. 118, 152

INDUSTRY TRADE SHOW

Trade shows occur every season and are used to show the new collections of the brands, or to show new fabric or trim developments. They are not usually open to the public, as they are for industry professionals only. › pp. 29, 165

KEY DATES CALENDAR

The key dates calendar drives the development and production process and enables all individuals involved to plan, create and produce a range. It is a series of deadlines (calculated by working backwards from the date the collection needs to be in the shops) specifying the dates by which the various stages of the process (design, fabric selection and ordering, proto review, launch, etc.) must be completed. › p. 220

LAB DIP

Lab dipping is a process for creating the designer's chosen shade in a chosen fabric by a colour lab (which works with the fabric mill) by mixing a series of basic dyes. This can happen at both the development stage and the production stage. › pp. 54, 60, 145

LANDED PRICE

The landed price is the total cost of goods for the manufacture, the freight and insurance up to the port of destination (where the goods are being shipped to). The calculation for the landed price is: FOB price multiplied by the Incoterm. › pp. 88, 128, 152

LAUNCH

The launch of a collection comes between the development cycle and production when the collection is shown to the sales teams and buyers. › pp. 15, 17, 88, 150, 164

LEAD TIMES

Lead time is the time between the placement of an order and its delivery. A fabric lead time can be anything from eight to twelve weeks, whereas trims can have a lead time of three to four weeks. › pp. 16, 62

LEG PANEL

A leg panel is one leg of a pair of jeans that has a pocket (in some cases) and all the correct stitching methods. It is used when the brand wants to see the effect of different wash or dye treatments, but doesn't require a full garment for this. › pp. 68, 132

LINE BOOK

The line book contains computer aided design sketches of the garments, and is a selling tool to help sell the range at launch. It contains the sketch, fabric information, colour offer, size offer and price. › pp. 19, 168

LINE LAUNCH

The line launch or launch happens at the end of the development period and is the first time that the collection is seen by the sales teams, buyers or public. The purpose of the launch is to sell the range. > pp. 15, 17, 88, 150, 164

LINE LIST

The line list is the key tool for all style information, and is used extensively by the merchandising team for sales. It contains the style name, style number, fabric and colour information, the FOB price and the gross profit margin. > pp. 19, 76, 87, 151, 155, 168

LOCAL MARKET FEEDBACK

Sales agents collect feedback based on their local views on their best and worst sellers, as well as relevant local trends. > pp. 145, 170

LOOK BOOK

The look book is a set of photographs of the collection either in the form of single garments or styled outfits. It is made by the brand and used as a selling tool after the launch. > pp. 19, 150, 168

MINIMUM ORDER

A minimum order can either be used for garments, fabrics or trims and refers to the minimum amount that needs to be ordered by the brand. Minimum quantities are set by the suppliers of goods and if these are not met by the brand, additional costs are calculated onto the cost of goods. > pp. 45, 57, 113, 170

MOCK-UP

A mock-up is a section of a garment that needs to be reviewed. Sometimes it isn't necessary to remake a whole garment to see a pocket, so a mock-up is made in the correct fabric and size for approval. > p. 166

PIECE DYE

Piece dyed fabric is dyed after weaving. Piece dye is the most widely used dying technique. > p. 54

PRE-PRODUCTION SAMPLE

A pre-production sample (PP sample) is the first sample in the production process, and is reviewed when changes are made to the salesman sample. > pp. 89, 103, 125, 156

PRODUCT GROUP

A product group refers to a garment type. > pp. 39, 45, 51, 119, 134, 152

PRODUCTION PLANNING

Production planning is the final stage of the information flow, and is managed jointly by the factory and the brand's production team. The planning sheet is a continuation of the line list. > pp. 16, 19, 88, 170, 176

PROTO NUMBER

A proto number is a unique identifying number linked to a designer's sketch. It is constructed in a specific way so that it is unique to the style, season, and product group. > pp. 78, 97

PROTO SAMPLE

The proto sample is the first fully made up sample of a garment made by the factory based on the designer's sketch and viewed while worn by a model. > pp. 63, 85, 94, 135, 145

PURCHASE ORDER

The purchase order (PO) is an official document drawn up by the brand for the factory or manufacturer, which states how many garments, of which colour and which size need to be made. It also specifies the price, delivery location and delivery date. > pp. 16, 104, 107, 176, 173

RANGE PLAN

A range plan is a table of information listing the quantity, types of garments and their prices to be planned and designed for a fashion collection. It is created by the merchandise team and is constructed from sales history, financial targets, local market feedback and trend information. > pp. 18, 36, 58, 120, 144, 170

READY TO DYE FABRIC

Ready to dye fabric is a fabric, which started off as greige and underwent a fabric finishing process to make it ready for use in piece dyeing or garment dyeing. > p. 54

RETAIL LINE

A retail line is a set of collections that are sold directly to customers through the brand's own shops, and can have between two and six collections a year. > pp. 17, 166

RETAIL PROFIT MARGIN

The retail profit margin is the percentage of the retail price that is the profit for the brand. The calculation for the retail profit margin is:

$$\frac{\text{Retail price} - \text{landed price}}{\text{Retail price}} \times 100$$

> p. 152

RETAIL PRICE

See 'Selling price.'

STYLES AND OPTIONS

A style is a single item of clothing like a jacket or a skirt, and an option is a colour way, wash or finish of a style. So, for instance, if a jacket is available in three colours, it is one style in three options. > p. 60

SALES ANALYSIS

Sales analysis identifies the previous season's best and worst sellers. Most ranges have best sellers every season, and at the start of range planning the merchandise team refers back to the previous season's sales figures to establish which styles can be continued to the next season with a change of fabric or colour. > pp. 45, 178

SALESMAN SAMPLE

The proto samples, once they have been completed with correct branding, fabrics and fit changes by the factories, become salesman samples. These are used for selling the collection to sales agents or stores. > p. 150

SELLING PRICE

Also known as the RRP (Recommended Retail Price); this is the price for which the garments are sold in stores. > pp. 39, 58, 146, 152

SIZE SET

A size set of samples is a set of three or more samples of the same style but in the different sizes. This is requested by the brand when it is important to see how the different sizes within the style affect the proportions of the style. > pp. 125, 157

SOURCING PLAN

The sourcing plan is made by the development team to decide which factories are used in which country and for which product group. The plan is made at the start of the season and can change during the development process. > p. 119

STYLE ALLOCATION

Style allocation is the process of deciding which factories get to make which styles. The style allocation is made after the sourcing plan is complete. > p. 119

TECHNICAL PACK

The technical pack, also known as tech pack, BOM (bill of materials) or GWS (garment work sheet), is a document produced by the development team informing the factory of all the details relating to a particular style. › pp. 18, 79, 113, 134, 144

TIME LABEL

A time label in a garment identifies the factory, the purchase order of the garment, the month and year the garment was made, and also the style number. › p. 104

TOILE

A toile is a version of a garment made by the factory to test a pattern. It is usually made in simple cotton or other cheap fabric. › p. 85

TOLERANCE

Tolerance is the amount by which a measurement for a garment may vary from that specified in the tech pack. Each brand has an agreed tolerance within which the factories must work for each measurement. › pp. 125, 135

TRIM

A trim is an additional item added to the garment to either enhance its appearance, for instance a lace or coloured contrasting fabric, or it can be a type of fastening. Buttons, labels, zips, rivets, snaps or hangtags are examples of trims, which the company uses to brand or identify its name. › pp. 94, 145

TRIM MOULD

A trim mould is a shell into which the trim material is poured or placed and is used in the manufacture of buttons, or metal tags or leather labels. › p. 96

WASH CARE LABEL

The wash care label informs the customer of the fabric composition and the washing instructions of the garment. › pp. 102, 125

WEIGHTED PROFIT MARGIN

The weighted profit margin includes the number of pieces in that style that have been sold. The calculation for the weighted profit margin is:

$$\frac{\text{Total sale value} - \text{total landed value}}{\text{Total sale value}} \times 100$$

› p. 158

WHOLESALE LINE

A wholesale line is a set of collections that are sold to shops and can have between four and six collections a year. They are launched at inter company line presentations, also known as line launches. › pp. 17, 166

WHOLESALE MARGIN

The wholesale margin is the % profit made by the brand on sales to shops. The calculation for the wholesale margin is:

$$\frac{\text{Wholesale price} - \text{landed price}}{\text{Wholesale price}} \times 100$$

› p. 152

WHOLESALE PRICE

The wholesale price is the price at which the goods are sold to shops. › pp. 152, 159

YARN DYE

A yarn dye fabric is one which could be either a stripe, a check or an all over pattern, woven from yarns that have been dyed to the colours required by the brand. › p. 54

USEFUL
websites

Whether you are new to the industry or have worked in it for years, it's crucial to bookmark industry websites, blogs or e-zines that keep you updated on process, designers or resources. These are some of my favorites that I use on a regular basis. Use these as a starting point and build your own private reference library.

> **Blogs and 'Zines**
Blogs and online magazines on
fashion and style

Dazeddigital.com
Businessoffashion.com
Thecuttingclass.com
Ashadedviewonfashion.com
Nymag.com
Style.com

> **Fabric and trim testing**
Industry testing facilities and advice

Intertek.com
Sgs.com
Testex.com
Cirs-reach.com
Iso.org/iso/iso_14000_essentials
Oeko-tex.com

> **Software**
For product lifecycle management
systems, pattern making, and general
business and accounting programs

Lawson.com/industries/fashion
Gerbertechnology.com
Lectra.com/en/index
Sap.com
Techexcel.com
Koppermann.com

> **Fairs**
A selection of trade fairs for
fabrics, prints, yarns and trends

Milanounica.it
Pittimmagine.com
Premierevision.com
Munichfabricstart.com
Breadandbutter.com
Magiconline.com
Expofil.com
Printsourcenewyork.com

> **Trend forecasting**
Trend sites, colours, fabrics,
silhouettes, books and online
services

Modeinfo.com
Mudpie.co.uk
Wgsn.com
Stylesight.com
Peclersparis.com
Scout.com.au
Esptrendlab.com

> **Careers and Schools**
For portfolio sharing, college
courses and online learning

Artsthread.com

> **Logistics**
For up to date information on shipping
terms and costs

Iccwbo.org/incoterms
Ftc.gov

> **Business resources**
For daily updates on the industry, fabric
developments, industry regulations, logistic
terminology and fashion articles

Just-style.com
Denimsandjeans.com
Fairlabor.org
Fairtrade.org.uk
Retail-week.com
Drapersonline.com
Wwd.com
Sportswearnet.com
Textilesintelligence.com
Clothesource.net
Fashionunited.nl
Textilia.nl
Journaldutextile.com
Fashion-dailynews.com

> **Twitter feeds**

General

@RAntoshak
@styledotcom
@Tmagazine
@modeconnect
@I_D
@CFDA
@BFC
@Lawontherunway
@FashionAdviceUK
@IAFnet
@Fashionunited
@FashionBizInc
@fashbrain
@Kfasanella
@SourcingJournal
@OSFashion
@Startupfashion
@AP_fashion
@fashpotential

Textiles

@iTextiles

Trends

@Trendstop
@TrendwatchingAP

Ethical Fashion and Eco Fashion

@EF_Coalition
@Ecotextile
@Magnifico
@RedressRaleigh

Manufacturing and Sourcing

@makersrow
@Cotton_Connect
@AATCC
@thecuttingclass

AUTHOR AND IDEA
Susie Breuer
www.co-lab54.com

EDITING AND DESIGN
Lilian van Dongen Torman
www.lilianvandongentorman.nl

COPY EDITOR
Stephen Breuer

PHOTOGRAPHY
Amsterdam Fashion Institute, Individuals
APXPRESS Ltd
Bill Tanaka
Breadandbutter.com
Calvelex S.A. Portugal
Lilian van Dongen Torman
Première Vision
Scarti-Lab - Mediterranean Manufactures; pictures by Tiberio Pedrini
The Victoria and Albert Museum London
Trey Guinn

ILLUSTRATIONS AND CAD WORK
Ehud Joseph
Sandy Chiu

CONTRIBUTORS
Mariette Hoitink, Peter Som, Costantino Ferrandino, Pauline Cheung, Nick Steele,
Damien Donnelly, Sandra De Gooyer, Melanie Tebbutt, Republic Models, Michael Arts,
Marco Araujo, Fabrizio Lupi, APXpress Ltd, Calvelex S.A Portugal, Andrea Eckersley,
Ehud Joseph, Sanne Laumen, Selma Kruimer, Marcella Wartenbergh, Lauren Fly,
Leonard Faustle, Jorma van Wissem, Loraine Redjosetiko, Lindsey Tramuta, Fiona Jenvey,
Martijn te Riele, Jane Grice, Saskia van de Kloot, Kirsten and Neil Schambra-Stevens,
Heidi Jales, Ali Hawkins, Felicia Irimia, Eddi D'Elia, Johannes Egler, Paresh Shah,
Tony & Melissa at Scarti-Lab, Lily Breuer, Sandy Chiu, Beno Bas, Mikki Engelsbel,
the students at Amsterdam Fashion Institute.

PERSONAL THANKS
The management at Tommy Hilfiger Europe B.V and Karl Lagerfeld B.V, Trey Guinn,
Rudolf van Wezel, Anneloes van Gaalen, Hannah Kruise, Samm Collins, Leslie Holden,
Anja Schuetz, Moony and Max Vitalis, Patrick Tissington and Suzanne Moore.

For Stephen Breuer
and Trey Guinn